GOD'S CONSTANT PRESENCE

True Stories of Everyday Miracles

Blessed *by* His Love

EDITORS OF GUIDEPOSTS

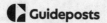

Blessed by His Love

Published by Guideposts
100 Reserve Road, Suite E200
Danbury, CT 06810
Guideposts.org

Acknowledgments

Every attempt has been made to credit the sources of copyrighted material used in this book. If any such acknowledgment has been inadvertently omitted or miscredited, receipt of such information would be appreciated.

Scripture quotations marked (CSB) are taken from *The Christian Standard Bible*, copyright © 2017 by Holman Bible Publishers. Used by permission.

Scripture quotations marked (ERV) are taken from the *Holy Bible: Easy-to-Read Version*, copyright © 2006 by Bible League International.

Scripture quotations marked (ESV) are taken from the *Holy Bible, English Standard Version*. Copyright © 2001 by Crossway Bibles, a division of Good News Publishers. Used by permission. All rights reserved.

Scripture quotations marked (GW) are taken from *GOD'S WORD®*. Copyright © 1995, 2003, 2013, 2014, 2019, 2020 by God's Word to the Nations Mission Society. Used by permission.

Scripture quotations marked (KJV) are taken from the *King James Version of the Bible*.

Scripture quotations marked (NASB and NASB1995) are taken from the *New American Standard Bible®*, Copyright © 1960, 1971, 1977, 1995, 2020 by The Lockman Foundation. All rights reserved.

Scripture quotations marked (NET) are taken from the *NET Bible®* (New English Translation). Copyright © 1996–2017 by Biblical Studies Press, L.L.C.; http://netbible.com. All rights reserved.

Scripture quotations marked (NIV) are taken from *The Holy Bible, New International Version*. Copyright © 1973, 1978, 1984, 2011 by Biblica, Inc. Used by permission of Zondervan. All rights reserved worldwide. zondervan.com

Scripture quotations marked (NKJV) are taken from *The Holy Bible, New King James Version*. Copyright © 1982 by Thomas Nelson.

Scripture quotations marked (NLT) are taken from the *Holy Bible, New Living Translation*. Copyright © 1996, 2004, 2007 by Tyndale House Foundation. Used by permission of Tyndale House Publishers Inc., Carol Stream, Illinois. All rights reserved.

Scripture quotations marked (TLB) are taken from *The Living Bible*. Copyright © 1971 by Tyndale House Publishers, Inc., Carol Stream, Illinois. All rights reserved.

Cover design by Serena Fox Design Company
Interior design by Serena Fox Design Company
Cover photo by © Klagyivik, dreamstime.com
Typeset by Aptara, Inc.

ISBN 978-1-961126-25-1 (hardcover)
ISBN 978-1-961126-26-8 (epub)

Printed and bound in the United States of America
10 9 8 7 6 5 4 3 2 1

By watching carefully our endless desire to love,
we come to the growing awareness that we can love
only because we have been loved first, and that
we can offer intimacy only because we are born out
of the inner intimacy of God himself.

–*Henri Nouwen, theologian*

TABLE *of* CONTENTS

———◆———

Magnifying God's Love

Eryn Lynum

I STARED AT THE ITEMS on the table and considered how to arrange them in my backpack. I would embark on an intensive, 3-day wildflower class in the Rocky Mountains the following day. Our lessons would take my classmates and me to mountain lakes, subalpine trails, and the tundra—a sparse landscape so high in elevation that not even trees grow, but apparently, as I would learn, wildflowers thrive.

I tucked a wildflower guidebook, snacks, a water bottle, a journal, and a pen into my day bag. Lastly, I added a small magnifying glass—much like jewelers use to inspect diamonds—into the pocket of my bag. Over the following 3 days, that magnifying lens invited me into a new world. Perhaps, more correctly, it invited me deeper into God's created world in a way I had never before experienced. As it would bring into focus the intricacies of God's designs, my vision of His ever-present love would grow sharper. And I would need that perspective a month later when I discovered a lump in my breast.

Intentional Pause

SOMETHING SPIRITUAL HAPPENS when one intentionally pauses and peers into nature's fine points. Elihu, one of the authors of the book of Job, understood this. In Job 37:14 (ESV), he wrote, "Stop and consider the wondrous works of God." When one pauses to contemplate how carefully God designed nature to thrive and how He tends to all He has made, His love becomes clearer.

Perhaps this is why Jesus, in His teachings, utilized the materials He and the Father fashioned at creation. Into His lessons, He integrated sparrows, stars, grains of sand, and olive branches to anchor truth in the minds and hearts of His listeners.

In Matthew 6:25–34, Jesus drew His audience's attention to birds of the air and flowers of the field. I've often pictured Jesus standing before the crowds, talking about birds and botany, all while wildflowers dotted the hillside and birds flitted above or pecked at seeds around His feet.

I wonder if a woman, while listening attentively to Jesus's words, bent low to examine the petals of a wildflower like I was now, up on a hillside on the tundra. I pulled out the magnifying lens and placed it close to the dainty, purple-blue petals of the sky pilot flowers. How had I never noticed them before? My family and I had explored this area along Trail Ridge Road— the highest continuous paved road in America, rising to 12,183 feet above sea level—many times.

We'd noticed the elk, of course. Even on this day, a couple hundred feet from my classmates and me, an elk herd lay sprawled on the sunny tundra, munching whatever ground-cover they could find. Perhaps I'd always been so busy looking at the obvious, like a herd of elk or marmots skittering across rocks, that I'd missed the wildflowers. They looked out of place—such fragile beauty in the harshest landscape.

A few hiking trails wind across the summits at this elevation. But there are vast stretches of wilderness that are rarely explored. How many wildflowers bloom and fade into time, never to be seen or admired by a human eye? And yet God clothes them in splendor.

I, too, can feel unseen. In my work, daily sacrifices, and fears, and buried beneath life's burdens, it's easy to feel alone in one's head, as if my worries and questions go unnoticed. Yet God places a magnifier on my thoughts. King David cried out in Psalm 139:23 (NIV), "Search me, God, and know my heart; test me and know my anxious thoughts."

And this is precisely what God does. As He places a magnifier over the thoughts of His children, He is not deterred. He is not caught off guard, repulsed, or wearied by my constant return to well-worn paths of fear or frustration. Instead, He examines my heart and draws my attention and affection back to Himself. In verses one and two, David opened the chapter with these words: "You have searched me, LORD, and you know me. You know when I sit and when I rise; you perceive my thoughts from afar."

The end of this verse has perplexed me in the past. I don't like to think of God "from afar." In Psalm 46:1 (ESV), I read of God as a "very present help in trouble." How can He be both very present and afar? Perhaps David simply felt as though God was far away. Maybe his fear skewed his perspective of how close God really was. Or perhaps "from afar" can relate to time rather than physical distance.

God stands outside of time, and He is well aware of my thoughts from a decade ago, yesterday, today, and what they'll be preoccupied with a year from now—or a month from now, when I would be sitting in a doctor's office after feeling the lump in my breast.

"It doesn't feel concerning," my doctor assured me. "It's probably only a cyst, but we can never be too safe with these things. I'll order imaging and an ultrasound just to be sure."

I knew I had a decision to make as I walked out of the doctor's office. Weeks of waiting and uncertainty lay ahead of me. The posture of my heart during that time would depend on what I chose to place a magnifier over.

I could fixate on the lump and my fear, trying to fill the void of the unknown with possible scenarios. Or, I could trust that God, who exists "from afar," already in the imaging room, knows every cell in my body because He engineered them before time began. I turned on my car to return home to my husband and four young children, deciding at that moment with a prayer to place the magnifier over God's ever-present love.

Birth of a Butterfly

THE IMAGING office called the following day to schedule my appointment. It would be 2 weeks before we had more information. As I practiced forcing fear out of my mind, I received another opportunity to take a magnified look at God's creation, this time not with flowers, but butterflies.

My children had been keeping a monarch caterpillar they found in our garden in a large jar, and it began spinning itself into a chrysalis. We saw him right in time to watch the entire process, which only took a few minutes.

The evening before, the caterpillar had sealed himself on the underside of the jar's rim by creating a silk pad. All night, he'd hung still in a *J* shape, and now he whipped into action. As he moved, a beautiful lime green chrysalis began to form, starting from his bottom and wrapping up to the top until he was completely enveloped. The chrysalis formed, hardening into a stunning, shiny shell with golden gems sealing the top.

This was one of five monarch caterpillars we were rearing. We'd missed the production of the first caterpillar wrapping itself up. However, over the following weeks, we'd witness three of the monarchs creating their chrysalis, and we'd also get to watch three of them emerge as butterflies. I'd never had such a close-up view of this magnificent process.

In the days before creating a chrysalis, monarch caterpillars are incredibly active as their entire job is to eat as much milkweed as possible. Then, once they had wrapped themselves up in their green blankets, and before any had emerged as butterflies, everything was still. It was strange watching them in constant busyness and then profound stillness.

Walking by, I would check on the chrysalis and note how they changed despite their lack of movement or activity. The chrysalis would turn from green to translucent on the day before a butterfly would emerge. We could see through to the vivid black and orange colors and patterns of the monarch butterfly's wings.

It was as if God had placed these monarchs in our garden to be reared in our home in that specific season to teach me an essential lesson about waiting in His love. Focusing on their stillness, I, too, could slow down and trust what God was doing in my waiting.

It struck me that although God designed the intuition into a caterpillar to wrap itself in a chrysalis at the proper time, the caterpillar cannot know what will take place. They never saw their mother, a butterfly, and have only known a life constrained to foot travel. I wonder about their first perceptions as they split open the chrysalis and take their wobbly first flight.

I wonder, too, about the days they spend inside the chrysalis. God created caterpillars with clumps of cells called imaginal discs. Only recently, with the development of magnification and microscopic technology, have scientists discovered these incredible designs bearing the Creator's fingerprints. Inside the chrysalis, nearly the entire body of a caterpillar liquifies, and those imaginal discs form into the new parts of the butterfly.

I wondered if God was doing a similar work in my mind and heart as we waited for a prognosis. Time and waiting open the gate wide for fear, yet God was inviting me to take every thought captive. It was an invitation from Psalm 27:14 (NIV) to "Wait for the LORD; be strong and take heart and wait for the LORD."

As our butterflies emerged one by one and took to the sky, I thought about how God was reforming my faith and making it new. Like the imaginal discs in a caterpillar, He'd placed into me long ago the potential to know His constant presence and love. Now, He magnified those perceptions and transformed my faith into something more robust and vivid. But this metamorphosis of faith would require me to remain in His presence and constantly turn my frenzied and fearful thoughts to His constant love.

A Close-up View

MAGNIFICATION HAS a profound effect on one's focus. It brings into view what couldn't be seen before. During my wildflower class, as I peered through the magnifying lens, I could see the tiny parts of each flower. I observed the small purple splashes inside a spotted coral flowerhead.

On an elephant flower, I could make out petals perfectly resembling elephant ears and trunks. I could glimpse the miniscule pollen tips extending from each flower head and the protective sepals wrapping around petals and securing them to the stem. It surprised me how many little pieces make up a single flower.

I have found a similar effect when I place a magnifier over God's love, and the details of His affection and devotion become clearer. I am as guilty as anyone of rushing through a recitation of John 3:16's familiar words. However, when I pause and look closer, I see what I didn't before. The verse (NIV) says, "For God so loved the world that he gave his one and only Son, that whoever believes in him shall not perish but have eternal life." Only as I narrow in on the Greek word for love, *agape*, do I see the intricacies of a willful, sacrificial, and pure love.

Just as a magnifying lens on the trail taught me to hike slower, searching out the fine points of God's love encouraged me to read Scripture more earnestly.

In Psalm 100:5 (NIV), I find His love's unconditional nature: "For the LORD is good and his love endures forever; his faithfulness continues through all generations."

First John 4:19 (NIV) reveals another detail of God's love: "We love because he first loved us." It is echoed in Romans 5:8 (NIV): "But God demonstrates his own love for us in this: While we were still sinners, Christ died for us." I can extract from these scriptures the unconditional attribute of God's love—that His love is holy, requiring Christ's sacrifice on my behalf, but also unconditional in that He came despite my unworthiness. His love seeks me out.

Ephesians 2:4–5 (ESV) brings into focus the mercy and restorative quality of God's love: "But God, being rich in mercy, because of the great love with which he loved us, even when we were dead in our trespasses, made us alive together with Christ—by grace you have been saved."

The Bigger Picture

WHEN MAGNIFYING the details of a flower, I was looking at tiny parts, but I quickly realized that I was also glimpsing a bigger picture. Every detail was a part of something more significant. This is especially true with composite flowers like those in the daisy and sunflower families. The center disk is composed of hundreds of individual disc flowers, and what I previously thought were petals adorning the disc's exterior are individual ray flowers.

Later at home, I would hold up a single sunflower head and ask my kids how many flowers I was holding. They looked at me as if I were joking and responded, "One." I told them I was holding hundreds of flowers. I used the magnifier to show them the individual disc and ray flowers within one sunflower head. Each tiny floret is a part of something bigger.

I see a similar design in the attributes of God's love. I glimpse a bigger picture as I focus on His willful, eternal, unconditional, holy, merciful, and restorative love. His love is not a part of His character—it is His very identity. First John 4:16 (NIV) says, "And so we know and rely on the love God has for us. God is love. Whoever lives in love lives in God, and God in them."

I can rely on God because He is love.

Finding Focus

MAGNIFICATION BRINGS details into focus while also pushing anything in the peripheral out of view. As I placed a magnifying lens over the details of flowers and butterflies, I found everything in the peripheral faded out of view. Whatever lay outside the black frame around the glass was forced out of the picture. God created human minds to work similarly. He designed the human brain to be flexible so that one can train and retrain thought patterns and take every thought captive.

As I waited for my next doctor's appointment, at times I could feel a heavy fog settling over a day, obscuring my view of the horizon. All I could perceive was fearful thoughts. I considered the caterpillars and felt like them, wrapped up without a view of the outside world. Then God would bring to mind

2 Corinthians 10:5 (ESV): "Take every thought captive to obey Christ." I would rein my thoughts back in and redirect them toward God's love. The fog would lift at once, and I could again see His faithfulness and tender care.

Surrender

TWO AND A HALF weeks after discovering the lump, I sat in a small waiting room after my examination. Down the hall, the imaging nurse reviewed X-ray and ultrasound images. I knew in a few minutes I would have answers. I fidgeted with my wedding ring in nervousness. I could sense the fog of fear creeping like smoke down the hallway, ready to enter the waiting room and consume me. Yet prayer kept it at bay.

In those minutes, I surrendered the outcome to an all-knowing and all-loving God. The waiting room became a magnifier, a time of waiting, much like a caterpillar in chrysalis, for an unknown future. And yet it was not wholly unknown, for God was with me and loving me "from afar"—from the future He fully knows.

"I have good news for you," the doctor began. She assured me the images had not revealed anything out of the ordinary and there was nothing to be concerned over.

Her words reflected what I'd felt on the tundra when I made a correct identification after studying a flower under the magnifying lens. Everything came into clearer view, and unknowns faded into the peripheral. It felt, too, like watching the vivid patterns of our monarch butterflies as they made their inaugural flights. I almost felt their surprise as their wings trapped air beneath them and pushed them toward the heavens. Like a fledgling bird, they wobbled awkwardly before gaining confidence and taking higher to the sky.

My faith felt similar as I walked out of the office into the bright sunlight. God had been transforming and growing my trust in Him in the waiting. I could confidently step into whatever came next, knowing that God can see beyond the fog and His blessed love reaches me from afar, where He is sovereign and in control.

Life is punctuated by these seasons of waiting, like a flower preparing to bloom or go to seed. And like a caterpillar undergoing metamorphosis, these chapters are not idle. God turns waiting into the fertile soil where faith grows and flourishes into something one could never imagine. Every time I sit with the unknowns of life, I can retrain my thoughts and create habits of magnifying God's love.

As much as I attempt to orchestrate a future I'm comfortable with, I cannot control the outcome. Yet I can rest assured that no matter what comes, God is doing something new, and His works are good. As I learn to trust Him in the waiting, I can place a magnifying lens over His character, pushing fearful or anxious thoughts out of view and bringing into focus the facets of His blessed love.

———— ◆ ————

God is connected to everything... The shells on the ocean shore, the mushrooms growing in the forest, the trees stretching to the clouds, the tiniest speck of snow in the winter, and *our dust-to-dustness*—we are all connected and tethered to this sacred gift of creation.

—Kaitlin B. Curtice, poet and speaker

CHAPTER 1

Divine Connections

Sew There

Linda S. Clare

Teaching special education was much more demanding than
I had expected. The year before, I'd graduated cum laude from
my university, but like many new teachers, I wasn't prepared for
the challenges of teaching middle school kids with disabilities. I
had a tendency to jump in and solve my students' problems for
them, especially if they struggled or took too much time with
a task. Still, I managed to muddle through my first few months
of teaching—until a student named Sharon came to class.

Sharon had cerebral palsy, a condition that affected most of
her motor skills. Cerebral palsy usually occurs during a difficult
birth, when the brain is cut off from oxygen for a period. Like
many with the condition, Sharon's muscles were spastic—as
if they were in a permanent cramp. Her hands were folded in
on themselves like claws, and she needed a wheelchair to get
around. Even her speech was affected, making talking very
laborious and hard to understand. But she had beautiful silky
blond hair, twinkling blue eyes, and a sharp mind. I took a liking to her right away.

With a brain that moved faster than the rest of her, she was
a very frustrated 12-year-old trapped in an uncooperative body.
She had temper tantrums when she couldn't do what she set
out to do. And when I met her, what she wanted to do was
learn to sew.

I asked her parents if there was anything else Sharon wanted to learn—sewing would be difficult for her and possibly dangerous given that it involved sharp needles. I wanted to steer her toward activities where she could succeed. Her mother shook her head.

"Sharon loves creating. She wants to learn to sew." Her mom laughed. "And when Sharon decides she wants to learn something, she's stubborn."

Well, I thought, *I'm stubborn too.* I was sure I knew best what a kid like Sharon needed.

> ## For nothing will be impossible with God.
>
> —LUKE 1:37 (NASB)

I gathered supplies for our first lesson: a large hoop and stand to hold her work, a large embroidery needle, thick red yarn, a length of tan burlap. I figured I'd have to do everything except punch a threaded needle though the fabric. Even then, I pictured guiding her fisted hand.

I threaded the large needle eye and knotted one end, showing Sharon how to grip the unknotted end to keep it from slipping out of the needle.

I demonstrated a running stitch. "See, Sharon? You go in and out, in and out. Do you want me to help you get started?"

Sharon's blue eyes turned stormy. With painstaking effort, she said, "I can do it."

I smiled. "Of course you can. Here, let me show you how to keep your thread from tangling."

She set her mouth in a frown as I prattled on. "Embroidery is sort of old-fashioned, isn't it? Why don't we think about doing something like iron-on transfers or splatter painting?"

Sharon glared at me. "My mom likes embroidery. I want to sew a heart." As she struggled to speak, impatience rose within me. I wanted to finish her sentences, to get on with it.

In my mind, I shrugged. *Have it your way.* But it was all I could do not to grab a pencil and draw a heart on her burlap. My discomfort only grew with her tortured movements. Things most people could do in seconds took Sharon much longer. But at long last she looked up.

"There. A heart for Mom." She grinned.

I stared at her effort. It had to have been the crookedest heart I'd ever seen. I shot up a silent, emergency prayer, begging God to give me the right response. Then a small voice inside me said this was no time to be quiet.

"Wow," I said. "That's a really great heart. Your mom is going to love it."

As Sharon handled the needle and thread, again I fought the urge to add pointers. *Not that way—see, you let the yarn fall out.* I wanted to do everything for her, but I knew she wouldn't learn except through mistakes. I had to pray again and again for patience. Somehow, I held my tongue and rethreaded the yarn over and over. Advice from the book of Job (13:5, NIV) came to mind: "If only you would be altogether silent! For you, that would be wisdom."

Over the next few weeks, she returned again and again to her project. It wasn't easy for either of us and required much prayer on my part, but I stayed silent while Sharon doggedly tried to follow the crooked heart's outline. Some days she managed only a stitch or two before she tired or threw one of her tantrums. Again and again, I felt God steering me toward silence when she botched the work.

But whenever she wailed in frustration, I began to learn what to say—and what not to say—to encourage my student.

"It's tough, I know," I'd say softly. "Take a break, then try again. You can do it—don't give up."

Sure enough, Sharon would rest, then attack her sewing with renewed zeal. Yes, it was slow going. But after a while, I began to notice that I was learning even more than Sharon.

I'd always been labeled a brain, a smart kid, a whiz. All through school, I'd aced my classes and would sulk if I made even a B. What I hadn't wanted to acknowledge was that besides the nickname of brain, I was also called a know-it-all. A big fat know-it-all who rushed to supply answers before most had a chance to ponder the question.

> Surely God is my help; the LORD is the one who sustains me.
>
> —PSALM 54:4 (NIV)

My impatience with anyone not as gifted as I was now stood in glaring neon letters. To be an effective special education teacher, I had to stop filling in blanks for my students or taking over just because something was easy for me. I needed to learn when to speak up and when to zip it.

While Sharon practiced sewing, I began practicing other skills. I paid more attention to the way I tend to blurt out information or correct others. I often failed to stop myself in time, blabbing when I ought to be silent, clamming up when speaking a kind word might have lifted someone's day. But little by little, stitch by stitch, Sharon and I both improved.

By semester's end, Sharon's embroidered heart was finished. Her masterpiece was still rather crooked, and her stitches often looked more like chicken scratches than embroidery. But one Friday when Sharon's mom arrived to pick her up, the girl beamed from ear to ear. She proudly presented her mother with the handiwork.

Her mom's eyes filled with tears as she gushed over her daughter's efforts. Sharon couldn't stop smiling as her mother praised her. "This is so beautiful! Thank you."

> **If any of you lacks wisdom, you should ask God, who gives generously to all without finding fault, and it will be given to you.**
>
> —JAMES 1:5 (NIV)

So many times, in teaching and in life, God has answered my prayers to allow others to discover their own solutions. Keeping my mouth shut prevents me from saying unkind or hurtful things. But when hurting people need encouragement, not speaking a good word can make sorrows worse. In school they don't teach you when to speak up and when to keep silent. But God has a way of pointing toward wisdom, whether we think we need it or not.

That afternoon Sharon straightened up in her wheelchair and declared, "I did it all by myself." Her mother glanced my way, seeking confirmation, and I nodded. Sharon indeed had overcome her physical challenges with grit and stubbornness. As her mom opened the classroom door to wheel her daughter out, Sharon stopped her.

"Wait." She handed me a paper heart, outlined in red. Sharon said, "You let me mess up until I got it. And you said I could do it. Thanks."

GOD'S GIFT OF SMELL
— Heidi Gaul —

EACH OF US POSSESSES a subtle personal scent that is solely our own. How many of us have held a baby close and breathed in their essence, aware that we'd be able to identify them with our eyes closed? It's the fragrance of kin, as powerful for our earthly family as for our heavenly one. "For we are to God the pleasing aroma of Christ among those who are being saved and those who are perishing" (2 Corinthians 2:15, NIV). God holds us close, smells Christ within us, and is pleased. We are His. He'd know us anywhere.

I took her gift. "Now that you know how to embroider, if you practice, you can do anything. I'm very proud of you."

Sharon fairly glowed with happiness as she exclaimed, "I can do it!"

I added silently, *Sew there!*

An Unexpected Bonus

Nancy Alvarez Yabut

The words brought anguish. "You're pregnant."

I longed for motherhood. But I was eighteen and had no means to care for a baby. I couldn't imagine how to make it work.

After I listened to the social worker's options for my baby at the pregnancy clinic, my brain fogged, and I stumbled out the door. My high-school sweetheart waited in his old green Chevy. His sobs broke my heart. How could we possibly raise a child? Should we put aside college and concentrate on providing for our rushed family? Or should we ask family members to care for the baby while we studied?

None of these choices seemed feasible or in the best interest of a child. Would it turn into a confusing conglomeration of caregivers? How would my relationship with my family be impacted? *Lord, forgive my disobedience. I should have followed Your ways. Show me the right thing to do.*

My pastor suggested adoption. The idea resonated with me. I prayed and discussed it with my boyfriend.

Reluctantly, he agreed. "We'll get married later and have more children."

The following months blurred by. Friends drifted out of my life. Family members voiced their opinions. Senior year ended on a melancholic note. Doubts flared, quickly replaced by a determination to do what was best for our baby—no matter the personal loss.

When the labor began, the terror of delivery ended with my baby boy whisked out of the room before I could catch a glimpse of him. Hours later, my fingers obediently signed the papers to sever our relationship. The final blow came when a foster family took him home.

The court hearing came and went. It was finished. I was no longer the mother of Baby Boy Kelley. Most likely, I would never see him again.

College began. A new start. Could I pretend having a baby never happened?

After 1 year of college, my fiancé told me he didn't want to wait to get married. I willingly put aside my college dreams and prepared for the wedding. Hope rose like the morning sun.

Months later, as I prepared wedding invitations for mailing, a letter arrived. My fiancé confessed that he was in love with another woman. Denial and disbelief bowled me over. I curled up on my bed and cried out to God.

> To all who mourn in Israel, he will give a crown of beauty for ashes, a joyous blessing instead of mourning, festive praise instead of despair.
>
> —ISAIAH 61:3 (NLT)

The Lord whispered a reminder of an earlier prayer. *Lord, if You want me to be a missionary instead of his wife, make him break up with me.* Whoa! I had almost forgotten that prayer. A ray of peace warmed me.

I lived in a haze for the next year, wiping aside the pain like sweat on a humid day. My longing for my son intensified. Yet, I never forgot my promise to serve the Lord overseas, and I worked toward that goal for the next several years. Eventually, God led me to the Philippines, and the thrill of being His ambassador turned my mourning into joy. I loved the country and the people.

Despite the satisfaction of helping others know Jesus personally, I still ached for my son. *Should I search for him? How? Would he reject me or welcome me? He would want to know his biological history, wouldn't he?*

Still, the daunting risk loomed in front of me. He'd be in his twenties by now.

A friend suggested I use the internet to find him. So, with trembling fingers, I typed his birth information on a website for adoption searches. Nothing showed up, no similarities, not even a remote possibility. Undeterred, I continued the search for 10 years before I finally set it aside to focus on my work in the Philippines.

At last, the Lord brought the right man into my life. We married and prayed for a child of our own. Infertility haunted me like an unwanted disease. The possibility that I wouldn't get to raise a child of my own made me yearn all the more to find my son.

Years later, we moved back to the United States. While we were living in Orlando, Florida, I renewed my quest. I needed to know if my son was happy. I asked an adoption counselor, "What's the best way to find my son?"

The answer was astonishingly simple. "You just need to pay three hundred dollars to the social service agency and they'll open his file. They'll reach out to him, and if he's willing, you can connect."

Chills trekked up and down my spine. With my husband cheering me on, I sent the check. Within 2 weeks, a social worker called to say my son had agreed to talk with me. Elation lifted me above the clouds.

By now, he was in his thirties. I waited for the call. Our first conversation was on Good Friday—it became Best Friday for me! We exchanged pictures, and the face staring back shocked me. *That's my son, no doubt.*

I didn't know how to respond when he commented, "I thought you were probably a prostitute or on drugs. You seem pretty together." Then he told me of his wonderful childhood and loving family. Relief and envy circled me.

> The LORD is a refuge for the oppressed, a stronghold in times of trouble.
>
> —PSALM 9:9 (NIV)

"What kind of work do you do?" I asked.

"I'm a choir director for my church, and I also play the organ for another organization. I sing opera and helped start an opera company."

"That's amazing. I'd love to hear you perform. You sure didn't get that ability from me." I enjoyed learning the details of his life. During another conversation, I asked, "Would you like to meet face-to-face?"

When he agreed, another thought entered my mind. Taking the plunge, I said, "Would you like me to find your birth father?"

"Yes, I'd like to meet him."

This audacious thought rattled me, but for the sake of my son, I decided to try. I sensed the Lord's nudge, but first, I would have to get my attitude straightened out. Fingers of resentment wrapped around me about the way my relationship with my former fiancé had ended. *Lord, help me forgive completely.* I scrounged around in my brain for an appropriate Bible verse to claim. I landed on, "Bear with each other and forgive one another if any of you has a grievance against someone. Forgive as the Lord forgave you" (Colossians 3:13, NIV).

Okay, Lord, I'll do it.

Back to the internet. I found his old address, where his parents still lived, and contacted them. Within days my ex-fiancé called. "I'm married and have four children. We're also fostering three kids with special needs. I'm so sorry for what I did to you. Please forgive me."

His sincerity melted away the years of bitterness. Healing flowed through me.

Later, my husband suggested, "Let's meet your old boyfriend and his wife. Maybe they'd like to hear about our ministry."

"You're asking too much. How could I face him?" I paused and rolled the idea around in my head. "Well, since I've forgiven him, maybe it wouldn't be so bad. Let me pray about it."

Once more I talked to my heavenly Father. *Can I handle something this scary? Do You want me to go the extra mile?* I again sensed the Lord's gentle prod.

We arranged a meeting. The couple invited us to speak to their home Bible study group about our mission work—and then spend the night in their home.

Really, Lord? I gritted my teeth and pasted on a smile. To my amazement, the awkwardness of that first meeting dissolved and gave birth to a real friendship—the unexpected bonus on top of the joy of being reunited with my son.

Our son now knows our medical backgrounds and the story behind his adoption. And he also connected with siblings, cousins, and grandparents. We delight in the relationship and marvel at his attitude of acceptance.

> **Your Father knows what you need before you ask him.**
>
> —MATTHEW 6:8 (NIV)

One time, our son told us he was going to perform at his church. We, along with his birth father and his wife, attended. His adoptive father joined also. When the adoptive father realized we were all together, he said, "She can stand to be in the same room as the birth father? I'm flabbergasted."

I could practically hear the angels in heaven singing "Hallelujah!" This testimony of forgiveness and grace spoke louder than any sermon.

Through all of this, I learned that, in His timing, God can take our failures, our disappointments, and our fears, and use them to bless us beyond all expectations.

Pennies from Heaven

Kim Taylor Henry

Taking a break from a computer project, I swiveled my study chair and gazed at my bookcase. My eyes landed on the long-familiar box containing the books of pennies that made up the collection my grandpa had started for me more than 60 years ago.

We lived on opposite sides of the country from my grandparents. In those days there were no cell phones, no texting, no emails. Phone calls were, for our family, an expensive luxury. So Grandpa wrote me letters, about one a month, from the time I could read, until he passed away when I was nineteen. In many of those letters, he enclosed a penny, its date handwritten on a small cellophane wrapper. I would place each one in the penny collection books he had given me.

Over the years, I made numerous trips to the bank to bring home rolls of pennies that I'd sort through and place in my expanding collection. I kept many of the duplicates, placing them in plastic bags with the year written in black marker. My collection grew to twelve books of pennies, more or less full, along with ninety-five ziplock sandwich bags of duplicates and a small pouch of loose coins.

Give it to Wyatt. The thought came suddenly, unexpectedly. I have three grown children and seven grandchildren. I could have given my penny collection to any of them. Yet, I'd never before even considered parting with it. It held too many special memories.

Give it to Wyatt. The thought persisted.

True, Wyatt, my 11-year-old grandson, had, not long before, showed me some quarters he had placed in a collection book. But that didn't mean I should give him my penny collection! I tried to push the thought from my mind.

Lifting the lid from the box, I flipped through the plastic bags. I dumped out the loose coins and spread them on the floor. I turned the pages of the collection books. Memories flooded back: Looking forward to Grandpa's letters each month. The excitement of finding the penny treasure inside and giving it a home in my penny books. Him sitting with me and showing me his collection when we were together. Other happy times with him. My pennies connected me to my grandpa, and I didn't want to let them go.

> **Whoever belongs to God hears what God says. The reason you do not hear is that you do not belong to God.**
>
> —JOHN 8:47 (NIV)

"Lord, is that You telling me to give this away?" I prayed aloud.

Give it to Wyatt. The thought came clear and strong.

Not long after, my husband and I were heading out for a Thanksgiving visit to see our son and his family. I placed the penny box and books in the trunk of our car.

"I'm giving them to Wyatt," I said. My husband, who knew I had been considering it, smiled. Thanksgiving evening, I took

Wyatt aside. "If you go get ready for bed now, ahead of the others, come into our room and I'll show you something I think you'll like."

It didn't take long for Wyatt, hair washed and slicked down, robe tied around his pajamas, to come into our room. It was just the two of us as I showed him my collection. He slowly turned the pages of the books, then lifted the lid from the box and surveyed the contents. I told him the story of how my collection had started and grown. He listened intently.

> **Do nothing out of selfish ambition or vain conceit. Rather, in humility value others above yourselves.**
>
> **—PHILIPPIANS 2:3 (NIV)**

Then I said, "If you want it, it's yours."

He looked at me wide-eyed. "I can't take it. You worked so hard on it."

"I love you, Wyatt, and I want you to have it."

"Really? You don't want it anymore?"

I laughed. "I want more for you to have it."

"But you worked so hard on it," he protested again as he continued to peruse the collection. Then he looked at me and grinned. "Thank you!" he said. As we hugged, I knew God had been right.

Early the next morning, Wyatt asked me to come into his room. The ninety-five bags of pennies were neatly arranged in rows on the floor. Our younger grandson was still asleep, so Wyatt spoke in a whisper. "I have a penny book too," he said, opening its sparsely filled pages. I hadn't known.

We spent a good amount of time looking through pennies together and filling some of the empty spots in his book. We talked about the steel pennies of the early 1940s and looked online for the reason for this deviation. He told me other penny facts I'd never known, like the four different reverse-side versions of the 2009 penny depicting parts of Abe Lincoln's life. He had a set, and he handed it to me to inspect. Again, I hadn't known.

Later that day, Wyatt showed his parents and siblings his new collection. He thanked me multiple times. I got more joy from giving my collection to Wyatt than the collection itself had given me for years. I would never lose the memories Grandpa gave me. And now, through God's prompting, and in His answer to my inquiring prayer, He was giving me wonderful new memories.

Ecclesiastes 3:1, 6 (NIV) says, "There is a time for everything, and a season for every activity under the heavens . . . a time to keep and a time to throw away." "Give, and it will be given to you" (Luke 6:38, NIV). The *Contemporary English Bible* translates this as "there is a time for . . . keeping and giving." *The Message* translates it as, there's "a right time to hold on and another to let go." The lesson I learned that Thanksgiving is that both those times can bring unimaginable blessings.

> **I remember the days of long ago; I meditate on all your works and consider what your hands have done. I spread out my hands to you; I thirst for you like a parched land.**
>
> **—PSALM 143:5–6 (NIV)**

The Blessing of Maria

Steve Watkins

I am at my desk, groggy after a sleepless night. The spreadsheets and editorial notes scattered about its surface are now irrelevant. Twenty-four hours earlier, I knew the fight was over. Despite hiring a dozen of the brightest minds in local publishing, my new startup business stares failure in the face, any prolonged agony spared by the choking forces of an economic recession.

Today we will shutter the business, launched just 6 months earlier, and stop the bleeding. It begins with the task of calling each of these talented writers and sales professionals into my office one by one and telling them to pack up their belongings because the vision I convinced them to share with me has collapsed. I am nauseous, but I stop thinking of myself because today is all about them. I must delay my own self-pity.

This is the worst day of my professional life. And at its conclusion, I find myself a failure. Broke, without hope, and absent any vision for what might be next.

Sitting at Gate 14, Terminal D in Memphis International Airport, I reflect on this day 3 years earlier and almost every day since, each day filled with chronic depression so bad that I still find it a chore to unload the dishwasher or even walk to the mailbox. I pray this experience just ahead of me brings me back to myself. This is the core problem, my mom tells me in our almost daily phone calls.

Son, you've just forgotten who you are.

This is how depression works. It robs you of your core identity and fills you with lies of unworthiness.

Today, my wife, Dana, and I have a one-way ticket to Guayaquil, Ecuador, bound ultimately for a new home in a small village called Puerto Cayo, just 1 degree south of the equator. We may or may not return, and we don't even really know what will determine that outcome. The inheritance of a small insurance policy from my father's death has made the change of scenery possible, along with our undefined dream of creating a missional outpost. And we know this is exactly what I need. A radical change of scenery. All the travel magazines say Ecuador is the "hot spot" for American expatriates to live well on a budget.

> **Walk in obedience to all that the LORD your God has commanded you, so that you may live and prosper and prolong your days in the land that you will possess.**
>
> **—DEUTERONOMY 5:33 (NIV)**

We are about to find out.

With three plane connections and a rental car, it is a long, but relatively smooth travel day, even though the 3-hour drive from the airport becomes 7 hours in the struggle just to find our way out of Guayaquil, a city of two million where there are no rules for driving.

We arrive at our new home just after midnight and I instinctively turn on the porch light for security in this new rural setting. The sleep is deep. But the next morning is a scene from a Stephen King novel. Thousands of crickets have crept into our home through a door facing that doesn't exactly fit. It's the onset of the dry season, and they are drawn to every water faucet and toilet. I spend the morning pushing mounds of crickets out the door with a push broom.

This begins day 1.

I have prayed not so much that this journey will take away my depression and all that accompanies it, but that it will restore the identity my mother says is lost. Her assertion is on point. Not only have I lost my identity, but I am no longer sure I care.

Puerto Cayo is a contrast and a paradox. Each evening, the sky is a spectacular canvas as the sun sets on the Pacific, with an array of colors that have no name. We sit atop our house, watching silently in awe of the peace it brings.

It is also an unforgiving land. The rural countryside's infrastructure, from roads to fresh water services to internet availability, is decades behind the US. Power outages occur daily and for hours at a time. Fresh drinking water is precious. If you can afford a vehicle, the good news is that the government-regulated gas prices are $1.41 per gallon.

The big surprise in this independent move we've made to become the hands and feet of Christ for the local population is that our frontline service group is a prominent population of Canadian expatriates. By droves, they are discovering Latin America's benefits and its climate, much improved over their Montreal winters. Most are atheists, but inquisitive about our faith in almost every conversation. The ministry opportunities have come directly to us.

If nothing else, in this new environment we are learning patience and a new standard for time—this is highlighted as we wait an entire week for our water delivery driver to search out the right screw and reattach an axle to his ancient tanker truck.

I first see her sitting on a palm stump at a small construction site on the beach just a half-mile north of town. She is looking over a drawing and barking orders to no one in particular. Born in Ecuador 50 years earlier, Maria Blount lived most of her life in New Jersey but returned to her homeland for retirement. Members of the small, local construction crew call her "la chihuahua" for her feisty spirit and for the way she gives directions on the site where her new home is under construction. The third time I pass her property, Maria waves me down as if I am a long-lost brother.

> So encourage each other and help each other grow stronger in faith, just as you are already doing.
>
> —1 THESSALONIANS 5:11 (ERV)

"Sit down and let's have a chat. I have seen you around," she says in unique English painted with Spanish and a touch of Jersey. It doesn't take so long to understand. I have discovered someone as badly in need of a friend as I am. Maria practically adopts my wife and me, teaching us the fundamentals of life in Ecuador. She travels to the market with us and is the first person to warn us of the "gringo tax" frequently placed on unsuspecting foreigners. She hosts us for dinner regularly. She takes us to church in an open-air building constructed with old cinder blocks, open enough that a few chickens pass in and out during the service.

In just a few weeks, Maria becomes a sister. She is a new presence in our lives, perhaps somehow sensing the difficulties we've experienced and always reinforcing just how much God values us.

When it comes to prayer, Maria is a force to be reckoned with. On a day when she finds me particularly sad, she grabs me by the shoulders and prays, almost shouting to God above and foreseeing a destiny filled with purpose. There is an informal dinner at her home that evening where I am surrounded by Maria's eccentric friend group. To my right is Mesfin, a retired Ethiopian businessman; to my left, Samuel, a retired Swiss seaman. I find myself laughing and leading the group in conversation.

> **I will instruct you and show you the way to go; with my eye on you, I will give counsel.**
>
> —PSALM 32:8 (CSB)

Just as I'm passing a plate of fried plantains, I somehow feel a moment of normalcy—the beginning of recovering my sense of self, of understanding who I am. Being surrounded by people with stories to tell draws me out of myself, reminds me that I'm someone who can help them tell those stories. It is not a grand revelation with the sound of trumpets and horns, but rather a subtle one that prompts a smile and some momentary peace.

Since Maria entered our lives, I am laughing again. I am thinking clearly again. And for the first time, I see a heavenly Father who is not looking down on me in disappointment. Scripture says God works in mysterious ways and in His own time. He used our yearlong Ecuador experience not to remedy every issue, but to prepare me for the next phase of my journey, a pilgrimage that would bring me face-to-face with myself and redefine my life in ways I never imagined.

I am unsure if God sent me 4,000 miles just to meet Maria so I might renew my sense of self. But this time in a beautiful and challenging environment made me confident that if we are pursuing the truth of our lives, He will use every circumstance for His greater purpose.

How Three Unexpected Friends Helped Mend Our Hearts

Sylvia Schroeder

When our daughter Charity first complained of a seeping numbness on her left side, none of us could imagine that within 26 days, a lesion on her brain stem would paralyze her. We had no idea our 26-year-old daughter—also a wife and mother to our grandchildren—could lose all ability to function as easily as if she had lost pieces of a puzzle. Doctors warned a "locked-in" state might reduce her to only eye movements. Now even those big blue eyes remained shut more than open.

Each new day grew into the worst day of my life. They piled together into long months of misery. Every day we prayed as the white-coated doctor leaned over her and said loudly, "Mrs. George, can you move your thumb for me?"

We would lean forward, all our eyes locked on her still thumb. Every prayer pleaded for a twitch, even a tiny one.

While Charity's health spiraled out of control, prayers grew desperate, petitions turned grim, time became an enemy. Friends gazed with pity and without hope on her unmoving form under stiff white sheets.

We pleaded for a miracle. Around the world, fervent supplications flew upward as people and churches heard about her illness. Despite those petitions, one look at her pathetic state brought disbelief and hopelessness.

Shock replaced the encouragement friends intended to bring. "Be careful what you pray for," well-meaning visitors cautioned after they saw her condition. Some even said, "It's time to let her go." Others avoided us altogether.

"Please, Jesus, heal her," we implored. We felt every prayer had been exhausted, every biblical charge met, yet each day she slipped further away. As seasons passed, the wounds of our hearts also deepened.

It was on one of those worst days that I first heard the whirring coming up from behind me. I was walking alone in the dim hospital hallway with my head down and my heart lower. Instinct told me I was about to get mowed down, and I turned to find a young man driving a power scooter. He abruptly slowed to maneuver around me, smiled, and then took off again as if the empty hallway were a speedway.

> Blessed be the God and Father of our Lord Jesus Christ, the Father of mercies and God of all comfort, who comforts us in all our affliction, so that we may be able to comfort those who are in any affliction, with the comfort with which we ourselves are comforted by God.
>
> —2 CORINTHIANS 1:3–4 (ESV)

I saw the paraplegic scooter racer again in the company of two others. A motley trio surrounded a table where they played cards. Another young quadriplegic man who used a power chair operated his machine through what looked like a long straw. An older woman sat on a walker, attached to a heavy tank of oxygen breathing life into her lungs. She picked cards for her friends from slim troughs that stood in front of them and laid them down. Her conversation, raspy and rough, came with effort. Their laughter and camaraderie filled me with a feeling I couldn't yet decipher.

Later, as I was sitting with Charity, I recognized it as dread laced with pure snobbishness. I deemed my daughter somehow better than this band of three. The bodies of these three had been irreparably broken, I reasoned, while Charity's was merely temporarily sick. She would get better. God would hear our prayers. Even though their abilities far exceeded hers at this time, I rejected with my gut a destiny such as theirs.

A child's voice drew my attention from where I sat next to Charity. Our 2-year-old granddaughter danced into the room. A pink tutu flounced at her waist.

"Mommy!" she shouted. Her arms spread wide, embracing the entire room, and her wake split the heavy gloom. She climbed up and over the hills and valleys of my daughter's prone body. I winced as little knees and elbows stretched transparent tubes and pulled at the skin where they were attached. Leaning down so her nose nearly touched that of her mother's, she sang "Be Thou My Vision." It was incongruous to see such a little girl comforting her comatose mother.

Her daddy stood framed in the doorway, a leather computer bag strap across his chest. In the crook of one arm, 6-month-old Bella slept motionless, like her mommy.

Where in all this heartbreak did prayer matter? Faith-tired and prayer-worn, everyone who loved her found themselves tangled in a wondering web of how to pray. We all felt somewhat paralyzed in a different way by the tragic events that consumed our lives.

I saw the three friends often during my hospital vigil. They traversed the sidewalks together, gathered to play games, and watched people come and go at the hospital's entrance. They seemed comfortable with their lives, and even happy in their own world, while Charity lay paralyzed, unable to talk and incapable of recognizing us.

I wanted a miracle, and I told God how it should look, shaping it with my own definitions. Thus, my prayers narrowed to exclude a disabled world that was incomprehensible to me, one to which my daughter now belonged.

> **I pray that God, the source of hope, will fill you completely with joy and peace because you trust in him. Then you will overflow with confident hope through the power of the Holy Spirit.**
>
> **—ROMANS 15:13 (NLT)**

My husband, facing his own internal grief, reached out to one of the trio one day while he sat in the waiting area outside Charity's room. The *whir* of a speeding scooter slowed as the vehicle neared him, then slid alongside him at the big brown table.

In the soupy fog of our grief, conversation took effort, yet curiosity took hold. My husband turned to the young man. "What is your story?" he asked.

In the next half hour, Luke⋆ talked about the car accident with a deer late at night that moved him from the walking world to the one our daughter had entered. Our worlds began to merge as first my husband and then all of us learned more about Luke. He could never again remain just an unfortunate member of the motley three. God's hand had moved our lives toward each other.

My son-in-law, ever the open and outgoing befriender, found the trio delightful. Interested in the stories of Luke, Drew, and Lucille, he invited more conversation. He seemed on a mission to destroy the barriers I'd constructed.

Until one day when a miracle happened.

Charity moved. Her thumb twitched. Small movements returned. Like pieces of a puzzle finding their connection, her lost abilities were finding one another again. Tiny reversals of divine awakening took place.

"It's a miracle," nurses said. Doctors didn't understand how or why the daily improvements were happening. Aides told me Charity's progress had become the hope of the entire hospital. Every day as I entered, the receptionist greeted me with some exciting new thing Charity had accomplished.

I didn't exactly forget the band of three, but I did put them on hold. They, however, shared in the excitement and anticipation of Charity's healing, asking about her daily and cheering her on. I harbored a protectiveness that wanted to separate her from their distinctiveness. I tried to keep her from the very ones who had begun to thaw a hard spot in my heart.

I didn't foresee how an unlikely trio of friends with disabilities could be part of God's answer to my desperate prayers, nor how God could use them to begin mending my own heart and preparing me for days ahead. But He did, and they did, starting with the day the miracle stopped.

Charity plateaued. She still could not sit up by herself, walk, or turn over in bed. I had not prayed for a halfway miracle. No one had. My prayers for Charity's healing rested more in the answers I prescribed than in the Healer Himself. They teetered on a hopeful outcome more than in the Person who is my hope. I'd given up my daughter to God's will many times over the months of her illness, and now I needed to do so again.

I was sitting in the window seat of an empty hallway when I heard the *whir* of his scooter come from behind. I brushed away the rivers of tears dripping off my cheeks. My back toward him and my face turned away, I stared at the outside courtyard.

> **He gives strength to the weary and increases the power of the weak.**
>
> —ISAIAH 40:29 (NIV)

Please don't stop, I begged in my mind. I willed him by me without turning and breathed a sigh of relief as I heard his wheels creep past. Then I heard him stop, do one of his turn-around-on-a-dime pivots, and come back. The *whir* ceased behind me.

"Come here," Luke said softly.

I shook my head, still not looking at him, but at his quiet command sobs burst from my soul.

"Come here," he repeated. I shook my head again.

He didn't budge. "Come on."

He was not going away. Without looking up, I walked to his scooter, leaned my head down to his shoulder, and bawled like a calf separated from its mother. Through my shuddering, I felt a small almost imperceptible *pat-pat* against my back.

"She's still your Charity," he whispered. "She's the same. I know."

Luke did know. He'd experienced it. From the vantage point of his power scooter, God began to show me a difficult yet glorious reality. God's ways are perfect, just, and right. He is the God of miracles who sees far beyond the boundaries of my vision and definitions.

Eventually, the time came for Charity to move on to a rehab center, but the motley crew remained in the hospital. Because our homes were about 6 hours away, we'd been staying with our son-in-law and granddaughters for several months in a rented house next to the hospital. As we packed up our accumulated possessions from our time living there, my son-in-law asked, "Is it okay to invite them all to lunch before we leave?"

Visions of choking hazards and oxygen mishaps filled my mind. I imagined death by pasta at the hospital's door. "Could you find out what they can eat?" I asked.

The day before our departure, our friends with severe disabilities sat around our table. One used a mobility scooter, another a breath-manipulated power chair, one a manual wheelchair, and an elderly woman sitting on a walker hooked to an oxygen tank forged a precious bond. My son-in-law, husband, and I pureed, mashed, and spoon-fed the diverse group.

As they laughed and joked about their disabilities, I recognized the acceptance and value of life they demonstrated. I realized the friendships I'd wanted to protect my daughter from were God's gift to all of us.

Sometimes God does not answer by parting the Red Sea or changing water into wine. Sometimes He answers with a gentle *pat-pat* on the shoulder, in laughter where it seemed none could exist again, and in communion with unlikely friends.

GOD'S GIFT OF HEARING
— Lynne Hartke —

THE SOUND OF wind rustling through the leaves has a fancy term: *psithurism*. It is adapted from an ancient Greek word, *psithuros*, which means "whispering." Whether the shaking of bright green aspens in the spring or the swirling of vibrant red maples in the fall, the wind moves through the trees, a reminder that God still speaks through His creation. His voice is not always the triumphant shout from mountains or the roar of a tumbling waterfall. Sometimes He speaks with a soft answer or a quiet murmur among the trees.

Hilarity and tears mixed at the "last lunch," along with a helping of gratitude. As I watched the banter, I thanked God for showing me His love through three precious, unexpected friends.

As for Charity, she was termed an incomplete quadriplegic and is in a power chair. She sees Jesus's love every day as she continues to embrace His will for her life. She has three children now, and her husband does an amazing job of caring for and loving them all.

★The names of Luke and his friends have been changed.

Jaenee, My Teacher

Beth Gormong

My own anxiety looked back at me from the eyes of the 16-year-old girl standing across from my husband and me at the airport.

"Jaenee?"

She responded with a smile and an affirmative nod.

"Welcome to Indiana." My husband reached for her suitcase.

What came next was an awkward introduction. *Do I hug her? Shake her hand? What is appropriate when meeting a stranger who will be living with you for the next 3 months? What would make her feel comfortable?* My husband and I had immediately volunteered when our pastor asked us to house Jaenee. But now I wondered if I was up to the task. It's easier to think about blessing someone than actually doing it.

I wish I could say I gave Jaenee the perfect welcome, that I hugged her like a mother would hold a long-lost daughter. But I was nervous and awkward, wishing for the perfect first impression, knowing reality fell far short.

We loaded her bags into the trunk and headed back home, an hour's drive from the Indianapolis airport. Small talk—well, any talk with strangers—is difficult for me, so I let my more extroverted husband and daughters take over.

Jaenee had flown from her home in San Diego to the Midwest for a worship internship at our church. She was young, adventurous, and brave. I was not.

We stopped on the way home for our first meal together...
Chinese. We had no idea what Jaenee's Filipino food culture
was like.

My mind raced. *Will she be offended? Does she think we think
she is Chinese or that Filipino food is the same as Chinese?* We had
so much to learn about Jaenee and her culture. I wondered if
she was secretly shaking her head at our ignorance of different
Asian cultures and cuisines.

Before we ate, we joined hands,
thanking God for the food and for
Jaenee's safe arrival. Holding hands
while praying marked the first
step toward blending Jaenee into
our family. Jaenee ate her Chinese
meal and thanked us for our gen-
erosity, and we headed home.

> ## As iron sharpens iron, so one person sharpens another.
>
> —PROVERBS 27:17 (NIV)

The long day of travel had
worn Jaenee out and I led her
to the nicest bedroom we had. We'd moved our girls into one
room and given Jaenee one of theirs. I'd cleaned and redeco-
rated it with robin-egg-blue paint and a soft flowered quilt.

*Was she comfortable? Did she need anything? Would she feel
welcome?* I worried and prayed, *"Lord, help me know and be what
Jaenee needs. Help her feel at home here. I'm not sixteen. I've never
been to California. I'm not Filipino. I'm so different."*

The next morning I set out the cereal and milk for breakfast. "Jaenee, what do you usually eat for breakfast?"

"Filipino breakfast rice. It's so good. Sometimes we eat it for
supper too. Would you like me to teach you, Auntie?"

My face must have shown my confusion, because Jaenee
explained, "Auntie and Uncle are terms of respect in my culture."

"Auntie. That's nice. I like it. Tell me what ingredients are in Filipino breakfast rice, and I'll make sure I get all the supplies you need today."

"Where's your rice cooker?"

"Rice cooker? What's that?" I had never heard of such a contraption. In fact, I'd never made rice before except for the kind that came from a Minute Rice box that I used in my favorite hamburger casserole.

When Jeff drove Jaenee to church for her internship, I researched rice cookers and made a Walmart run. Every Midwest home has the required eggs and oil, but I needed to pick up rice, onion, broccoli, garlic cloves, and soy sauce . . . and a rice cooker.

That evening we had breakfast rice for dinner and it forever changed my relationship with rice. My house smelled of sautéed garlic and onions for the first time. When Jaenee mixed fried eggs, cooked rice, crunchy broccoli, and soy sauce into the skillet, the smells she created were heavenly. And being her student in the kitchen helped break down the wall of awkward politeness.

"Jaenee, this tastes amazing. How about tomorrow night I make our favorite meal, hamburger casserole?" I thought she might like to experience a Midwest meal too.

"Okay, Auntie." She smiled politely but looked skeptical.

"Don't worry, I know you'll love it. It's so good." I gushed, ready to share my farmer's wife recipe with this California teen.

The next night I set the casserole on the table. After prayer, Jaenee dipped the serving spoon into the Pyrex dish and pulled out a serving. First she smiled, then she began to laugh.

"I thought hamburger casserole had actual hamburgers in it, like from McDonald's. You should call it ground-beef casserole,

Auntie." She took a big bite and proclaimed it good . . . much better than a McDonald's hamburger casserole.

This sweet girl taught me a lesson in graciousness. She was willing to try a scary-sounding casserole out of respect for her elders.

Over the next few weeks, we would experience other cultural miscommunications that led to laughter and confusion.

Take, for instance, the first morning it snowed. Jaenee had never driven in snow and was apprehensive about the drive to church.

"It's no big deal. The snow won't stick. The temperature is high enough that it's melting as it hits the ground. Just think of it as driving in the rain."

> **In the same way, let your light shine before others, that they may see your good deeds and glorify your Father in heaven.**
>
> **—MATTHEW 5:16 (NIV)**

She looked at me, even more terrified.

"What did I say wrong, Jaenee?"

"Auntie, when it rains in San Diego, the streets get really slick from the oil."

I had no idea my words meant for encouragement would cause greater dismay. "Okay, then that was a bad comparison. Trust me. It's not slick."

One evening Jaenee pulled knitting out of her bag. My eyes lit up.

"Jaenee, I've always wanted to learn to knit! Would you teach me?"

"Sure, Auntie. Come sit by me." She patted the cushion next to her. I slid in close and watched, mesmerized, as she clicked the needles, magically creating fabric with just one strand of yarn. Each evening Jaenee and I sat, heads huddled together, as she taught me the stitches needed to knit a washcloth.

"Auntie, I found a yarn shop on Wabash Street." Soon the shop became a favorite hangout and knitting a beloved pastime.

> **Be devoted to one another in love. Honor one another above yourselves.**
>
> —ROMANS 12:10 (NIV)

When Jaenee left to fly home, we hugged long and hard. Saying hello had been difficult, but not as hard as saying goodbye.

When Jaenee entered my life, I assumed I would be the mother figure who cared for a teenage girl. But God flipped my idea upside down, making Jaenee my teacher. She taught me how to be a good host, a better cook, and, most of all, a considerate friend. Our differences in age and culture weren't barriers; instead they acted as blessings as we learned from each other. Jaenee broadened my world by sharing hers with me.

Always with Me

Mark A. Brady

In most homes where an older person lives, there is often a spot, sometimes in the TV room, where the eldest member of the family always sits. This was the case in the home where I grew up. For a while, it was the couch. You didn't dare sit or lie on it when Dad was home, because it was his spot. As time went on, Dad preferred a recliner. It didn't take him long to realize he could drop off to sleep as easily there as on the sofa.

Toward the end of his life, his spot became a soft, textured, baby blue recliner. The table next to him held his remotes—which he always got mixed up and then would wonder why the TV wasn't working right—a lamp, a magnifying glass, his Dallas Cowboys thermal cup, and his phone. "Baby Blue" lined up with the TV screen in perfect harmony. It was Dad's spot . . . his chair.

I was in Dad's house by myself several times after he passed away. Even though he was no longer there, I couldn't bring myself to sit in his chair. I'm not sure if it was out of respect or because he used hair products that stuck on the towel he kept on the headrest. Then, one day while I was there, I decided to throw away that towel.

We had decided to hold an estate sale after everyone got whatever reminders of Dad he or she wanted. No one took Baby Blue. I'm not aware of their reasons, but I didn't particularly like recliners either. And the color of the chair wouldn't go with the rest of the motif in my living room. But the main reason I didn't want the chair was that it reminded me too much of Dad.

We had shared too many conversations while he was sitting in his chair, his spot. Some I would rather not remember. Some got too loud, and too many hurtful words were spoken.

> **Bear with each other and forgive one another if any of you has a grievance against someone. Forgive as the Lord forgave you.**
>
> —COLOSSIANS 3:13 (NIV)

I loved my father very much. He was a very hard worker. He was amazingly friendly. It was as if he personally knew everyone shopping at Walmart on any given day and wanted to catch up with him or her. He could fix most things. He provided for the family's needs and was the greatest fisherman I have ever known. The last three times my father and I went fishing, we kept all our catch.

The best thing, though, that my father did, along with my mother, was to take us to church faithfully. We seldom missed. In fact, some of my first memories are sitting on the back pew of a church. I heard the gospel and accepted Jesus Christ at a very young age.

So from my father I learned how to fish, spend time with people, and be generous. I learned to be a faithful, loyal, and hard worker. But putting his chair, his spot, in my house and perhaps making it my spot was not the way I wanted to remember him.

One day, while I was working at Dad's house and preparing for the estate sale, I heard a voice say, "Go sit in your father's chair."

I knew it was direction from God, but I wouldn't do it. "No, God. Sorry, but I don't want to." The thought of sitting in Dad's spot was too much.

The last night I was in the house, I heard God once again tell me to sit in my father's chair. This time, though, the message was a little louder and more forceful.

I went to the recliner and sat in it. It felt as if Dad had sat in it for so many years that the chair had formed to his body.

I didn't know what to do next. I closed my eyes but knew I wouldn't fall asleep. Then I said to God, "Okay, God. I'm sitting in Dad's chair. I'm in his spot. Now what?"

> **But the wisdom that comes from heaven is first of all pure; then peace-loving, considerate, submissive, full of mercy and good fruit, impartial and sincere.**
>
> **—JAMES 3:17 (NIV)**

After a few minutes, I heard the Spirit of God whisper, "Your father was the patriarch of this family. He ruled with unresolved hurt and pain in his own heart. But now you are to be the patriarch of the family, and you are to rule with love, forgiveness, and peace."

I sat there and cried. My family did need a lot of healing, a lot of prayer, and a lot of love. So I accepted God's decree, but I knew I would need His help, patience, power, and might to be the type of loving, understanding patriarch He desired.

A patriarch is the oldest member of a group but he is also a person who is the founder of something. I preferred the second definition. I wanted to start a new way for my family members to love, speak, and react to one another. I wanted them to show respect.

> **Whoever fears the LORD has a secure fortress, and for their children it will be a refuge.**
>
> —PROVERBS 14:26 (NIV)

As I sat in my father's chair, I was comforted in the loss of my father. Perhaps what God had shared with me were the same goals He had set out for my father as well. These were good goals for any family to have, and now my family would have an opportunity to live in them.

We did have the estate sale, but no one bought Baby Blue. I laughed as I told God, "No, I'm still not taking this chair and putting it in my house."

I moved it into the garage, and it sat there for a few days until I convinced a young man to take it for free. I persuaded him to take the chair by bragging on its color and showing off its functionality. I told him it would feel good to come home from a long day's work and relax in his new chair, and that all would soon know it was *his* chair, *his* spot. I pray the young man will be a patriarch after God's own heart for his family.

Baby Blue may be gone, but I will always have the memories of my father sitting in his chair, in his spot. Thank You, God, for using Dad's chair to speak to my heart and direct my steps. Your spot is forever in my heart.

When a Freezer Warmed My Heart

Shirley E. Leonard

It should have been a simple task. All I had to do was donate frozen vegetables for the soup sale. I was happy for an easy job in a church that was new to me. After over 40 years in ministry, we'd retired, and this pastor's wife found herself at loose ends in a new church.

I loved the music and preaching, but I sure didn't feel like I truly belonged. During my decades as the pastor's wife, I became a sort of mama or grandma to many, and I missed that feeling. People had opened their hearts to us. To me.

For the last 17 years before we retired, I was also the administrative assistant, with my own office at church. When I wasn't doing bulletins or newsletters, I was often listening to someone's deep need and letting God's grace take over when my wisdom ran out. It ran out a lot. Watching what the Father could do was an honor. I was humbled to have people tell me how much I helped them, just by being there.

But this was a new season and I had to adjust. I couldn't expect people I'd just met to treat me like parishioners had for so long. I was just another face in the pews now. So when the call came to donate for the soup sale, I figured, *Why not*? Maybe it would be a tiny step toward settling into church family life. *Such a small effort shouldn't be a big deal*, I thought.

Getting out of the house early so I could make it to church on time—check. Finding big packages of frozen veggies at the grocery store—got it. Getting to church with time to drop them off before the service—no problem.

> **Come to me, all you who are weary and burdened, and I will give you rest. Take my yoke upon you and learn from me, for I am gentle and humble in heart, and you will find rest for your souls. For my yoke is easy and my burden is light.**
>
> **—MATTHEW 11:28–30 (NIV)**

But finding somebody to tell me where to put my donations wasn't so easy. I asked a few people who smiled warmly but had no clue. A little girl showed me to a darkened room, but I didn't think that was the right place, and then she disappeared. Time was ticking. I didn't want to be late for Power Hour, our contemporary worship service.

This church was already big with a large kitchen, then they built an addition with a new, even bigger kitchen. There were multiple refrigerators. I checked them all, but none of them had any frozen veggies in the freezer compartments. And they were all pretty full. My search continued.

Then I remembered that the woman who called mentioned a walk-in freezer. I went back to the place the little girl had pointed to in the dark and found the light switch. I tried the door and walked right in. I found the bin of other bags of vegetables and added mine.

I turned around to leave and found the door closed—and locked. I kid you not.

Scenes flashed through my head from sitcoms and detective shows where getting locked in a freezer didn't end well. I took a deep chilly breath and prayed for calm. I saw a sign that said, "If you find yourself locked in, turn the knob a quarter turn and it will open." I carefully turned the knob, which was on the wall and not the smooth door, a quarter-turn, but nothing happened and there was nothing to grab to pull the door open. I tried the knob over and over. Nothing.

> Whoever conceals their sins does not prosper, but the one who confesses and renounces them finds mercy.
>
> —PROVERBS 28:13 (NIV)

I checked my phone, hoping I had cell numbers for any of my new acquaintances at the church. Nope. By now, 10 minutes had gone by and my earache-prone ears were starting to complain. Then my phone died.

I had a serious talk with the Lord, reminding Him that I needed His wisdom. I was leaning against the door in frustration when I tried the knob again. Bingo! Freedom, followed by relief and embarrassment. How had I not figured that out sooner? *Push,* don't pull. As I walked from the kitchen into the hallway, I asked God, "What was that all about?"

Even before I entered the room where the contemporary service was underway, I began to have a clue. I'd been feeling locked in for a long time by an unhealthy habit. What did this minister's wife do when no one was looking? Drugs? Pornography? Nope, nothing so dramatic. I snacked before bed. Every night. You may not think it's even worth thinking about. Or reading about. But for me, that silly, unhealthy rut had kept me in its grip for years. I'd made so many unsuccessful attempts to stop that I felt like a failure.

> If they listen and obey God, they will be blessed with prosperity throughout their lives. All their years will be pleasant.
>
> —JOB 36:11 (NLT)

As the leader asked us about our week and asked volunteers to share, I felt a new freedom to try to be myself, even though most of the faces were new to me. Although I knew God was with me always, He had used those icy moments to get my attention. I needed to break a habit that had been frozen solid in me for way too long. When it was my turn, I told them about my freezer adventure and the things God was showing me.

And suddenly, as I opened my heart to that small group, I felt less of an outsider and more of a part of a new church family. Once I admitted my weakness, stories flowed around the circle. People opened up and shared their own struggles with a variety of habits and attitudes. No one was judged, and I watched as members who'd shared worship for years discovered new things about one another. I knew in that moment that I could move beyond being a pastor's wife. I could simply be me, Shirley—a lady who got herself locked in a church freezer and unlocked her heart.

GOD'S GIFT OF TASTE
— Heidi Gaul —

LIKE THE DIFFERENT parts of the body the apostle Paul named in 1 Corinthians 12, the five senses are necessary for both survival and quality of life. And just as the eye needs the hand mentioned in verse 21, our sense of taste cannot fully function without the sense of smell. But we learn in verse 22 that the very parts seeming to be weaker are indispensable. Like the body of the church, each sense works together with another, to our benefit and delight. The sense of taste's unique need for assistance makes it all the more miraculous.

In the process of writing this story, God reminded me of the victory I had come to take for granted. It had been so long since the before-bedtime eating had stopped that I'd forgotten it was once a big deal. Apparently, God had unlocked multiple places in me while I was shivering in that church freezer. Remembering those minutes warms my heart.

And—just so you know—these days that church freezer has a new sign that says simply, "Push to open."

For a field to bear fruit, it must occasionally lie fallow. And for you to be healthy, you must rest. Slow down, and God will heal you. He will bring rest to your mind, to your body, and most of all to your soul. He will lead you to green pastures.

—Max Lucado, pastor and author

CHAPTER 2

Healing Body and Soul

The Small Lutheran Church

Jeannie Hughes

Snowflakes melted as they hit the windshield of my open-bed truck, trickling down the glass and looking like tears, mimicking my mood. My daughter and I were traveling from our West Virginia home to Ohio. Being a ceramic artist, she had ordered a new kiln for her pottery. Her works of art were beautiful, and they were selling as quickly as she could create them.

We had been going through a rough patch for what seemed like weeks. I knew I was the problem. I had become a dreaded helicopter mom. She seemed so young and innocent to me. I thought I knew what was best for her and wanted her to learn from my mistakes, to avoid making the same ones I had. My imagination ran rampant, playing out the what-ifs in my mind.

My daughter, on the other hand, had no doubt that her Lutheran upbringing would guide her in making the right choices. She needed me to let go so she could grow as an adult.

The tension had put distance between us. "Please just talk to me!" I wanted to cry out. But the only sound was the cadence of my wiper blades shoving the melting flakes to the sides of the windshield.

Thankfully, we had no problem reaching our destination—the GPS took us straight to the shop. The men from the shop loaded the large red kiln into the bed of my truck. My daughter was excited to get it home. I would be glad, too, as I hoped the plastic-covered kiln was properly tied down. I tried not to imagine the 290-pound kiln toppling out of the truck.

I was relieved as I smoothly guided the vehicle up the entrance ramp, mingling with other highway traffic. Then it happened. A detour sign instructed travelers to follow the arrow, pointing us in a new direction. The only sound coming from my GPS was "Turn around when possible."

Oh no! Oh no! I chanted in my mind. To my daughter, I said, "We'll just keep going. The road will eventually lead us home."

Finally, my GPS calculated another way to reach West Virginia. I followed the map it laid out for us, having put all my confidence in the directions I was given.

> **For the Son of man is come to save that which was lost.**
>
> **—MATTHEW 18:11 (KJV)**

An hour clicked by as we traveled along back roads. The snowflakes were falling faster now, and I worried I would have trouble driving my truck on the snow-covered roads. My tire tracks were the only indication someone had traveled this way. I had no idea if we were still even in Ohio.

Carving our way over the steep hills, I had to admit it. I was lost. The GPS was showing no existing road and sat unresponsive on my dashboard. I checked my phone, but there was no cell phone service. I felt cut off from everyone.

"I think we're lost," my daughter said. I felt like I was lost in so many ways in my life. "You always say all roads connect. You'll find a way," she said.

I wasn't so sure—about me or where we were headed. I thought about turning around, but at this point, I didn't even know if I could find my way back. At least we were talking as we always used to. The tension had dissipated in our common bond of not knowing where we were.

> **Walk in obedience to all that the LORD your God has commanded you, so that you may live and prosper and prolong your days in the land that you will possess.**
>
> —DEUTERONOMY 5:33 (NIV)

I started trying to make deals with God. *If You let me find my way, I'll stop trying to run my daughter's life,* I promised God. *Stop it! Stop trying to make deals with the Lord like a small child,* I screamed inside my mind. I needed to just try to relax and have faith we would eventually make it home.

As we crested a hill, we saw a sign on the side of the road: "Smallest Lutheran Church." My daughter and I looked at each other. Since we were members of our Lutheran church back home, there was little doubt we had to stop.

I slowly pulled the truck onto the gravel lot. No one else was around, but the stillness seemed comforting. I didn't once think of the danger we could be in. Two females, alone in the middle of nowhere. Our attention was solely on the small church. I was surprised to find the door was unlocked. We entered the wooden building, and it was as though we had stepped back in time. Four pews sat before us, just waiting for parishioners to show up.

"Oh, Mom, look at the pulpit with a podium for the pastor. I can just envision him saying, 'Peace be with you,'" she whispered. We sat on the front pew, its wood glistening as though it had just been polished.

We were silent, both of us lost in our own thoughts. In the stillness I prayed, thanking Jesus for allowing us this opportunity we would never have had if we hadn't gotten so lost. I prayed for guidance to get us home safely, to help us find our way. Not just to show us the roads home, but also to help us find the way to heal our relationship.

As we left the peaceful sanctuary, we noticed a guestbook and a donation box on an old wooden table in the narthex. My daughter signed our names, and we left a donation.

> **The LORD gives strength to his people; the LORD blesses his people with peace.**
>
> **—PSALM 29:11 (NIV)**

"No amount of money could be enough for such a wonderful experience," I said.

As we pulled out of the lot, calm settled over us. Somehow just being in the small church seemed to make everything all right. The snowflakes had stopped, and the air was fresh, as though I was being given a glimpse of the blessing we had just encountered. We could hear the gravel crunching beneath the tires. The hill we had been climbing began leveling out. The road opened up, becoming wider.

"There's a road sign!" my daughter said.

As it came into view, we could see it was a sign with an arrow directing us to the highway. I took a deep breath.

GOD'S GIFT OF TOUCH

— Buck Storm —

I NEVER LEFT my grandfather's house without a hug. Not just any hug—a big hug and usually more than one. They were "You are loved" hugs. And I definitely got the "I know you're a long way from where you should be but I love you anyway" hugs. Through those simple often wordless times of touch, my grandfather showed me unconditional and overwhelming love.

My grandfather is gone from this world now, enjoying his eternal embrace. But his love is not gone. I can still feel his arms around my shoulders, often when I'm least deserving.

To me, a hug is one of God's greatest miracles of touch.

"Oh, thank You, Lord," I said out loud. I reached over and gently squeezed my daughter's hand.

I felt so relieved, and knew God was directing me in more ways than one. If I hadn't gotten so lost, my daughter and I never would have experienced the healing peace of that small Lutheran church. And that was so worth the extra hours it took to find our way home.

Trapped on Windrock Mountain

Patricia Hope

My husband, Chuck, and I were arguing again. That's all we did these days. Money, the kids, our jobs. It didn't seem to matter. We couldn't agree on anything. Now we were standing in the middle of nowhere on the top of Windrock Mountain, 20 miles from our East Tennessee home, on a deeply rutted dirt road that had been neglected for decades.

A few hours earlier, we'd decided to take a drive and then go to lunch. Out of the blue, Chuck said, "Let's drive up the old Windrock Road and pick blackberries."

I could barely disguise my shock at his suggestion.

"Now?" I asked. I brushed my hands over my white crop pants and looked down at my sandals. I had bought them a few days ago and had my nails done so my toenails would look nice when I wore them. "I'm not really dressed for berry picking. If I'd known this is what you meant by a drive, I'd have worn something different. I don't want to ruin my good clothes."

"Come on," he cajoled. "Where's your sense of adventure? We haven't picked blackberries in ages. It'll be fun, just like when the kids were little."

Reluctantly, I agreed and even began enjoying myself as Chuck steered the truck up the deserted road. Nothing was left of the old coal-mining town except crumbling home foundations, but the vistas were beautiful. Chuck had grown up near Windrock and it held a special place in his heart. And he was right about the blackberries. The roadsides were choked with briars and brambles. Even from the truck, we could see countless berries already ripened to a deep black and purple.

The late July heat blew in through the truck's open windows as we zigzagged up the mountain. Chuck steered to the side of the road near the top, and we climbed out of the truck. "What are we going to put the berries in?" I asked, barely able to refrain from putting my hands on my hips.

He pulled a beat-up orange bucket from the back of the truck, shook out some leaves and debris, and grinned. "This ought to work." He walked over to a nearby bush and began gathering handfuls of berries, popping some into his mouth and dropping others into the bucket. His hands were soon covered with inky stains, and I couldn't help but think how I didn't want the same to be true of my slacks.

"These will make a great cobbler," he said.

Instead of agreeing, I shot back with criticism. "We won't have enough to bother with if you don't stop eating them." I picked a few berries as sweat poured down the back of my neck. My armpits were soaked, and my blouse was sticking to me.

> **For I am the LORD your God who takes hold of your right hand and says to you, Do not fear; I will help you.**
>
> —ISAIAH 41:13 (NIV)

"Chuck, I want to go now," I said in the least whiny voice I could muster.

He turned to look at me. "When did you stop liking everything?"

"I haven't stopped liking anything," I replied. "But we were supposed to be going out to lunch, remember? Not picking berries in this sweltering heat."

He swiped a hand across his face and then studied me. "We used to be spontaneous. And you liked it."

I looked down to see that my pants, indeed, had a purple stain across them. And dirt on one side. No telling how many ticks and chiggers had already burrowed into the bare skin on my feet and ankles. It's a wonder I hadn't already encountered a rattlesnake. I stalked back to where the truck was parked. I swung into the truck seat and slammed the door.

"Can we leave now?" I said through the open window.

"Okay," Chuck said. "We'll leave." He placed the bucket in the truck bed. "But just for the record, I don't think you like doing anything with me anymore."

I felt my cheeks flush. "Of course I like doing things with you. I just wish you wouldn't always go off plan."

Chuck climbed into the truck and cranked the engine. "See? That's what I mean. It's like we have to live every minute of our lives according to a script." He bumped the truck forward to the end of the main road and pulled onto a side road to turn around. He shoved the gearshift into reverse. "I don't want to plan every minute of my life, no matter how important you think that is."

He mashed the accelerator, but the truck didn't move. We could hear the wheels spinning. "I can't get any traction," he said, a note of dismay in his voice. He put the truck in Park and opened the door to get out.

I opened my door and got out, too, furious at him for putting us in this situation and furious that he'd brought us up this horrible mountain in the first place. How would we ever get out of here? We didn't have four-wheel drive. We didn't have a cell phone, because such a thing hadn't yet been invented. We didn't even have drinking water, and I knew—even without a thermometer—that the temperature was already in the nineties.

> **My dear brothers and sisters, take note of this: Everyone should be quick to listen, slow to speak and slow to become angry.**
>
> —JAMES 1:19 (NIV)

"We'll have to go down this road," Chuck said. "I can't back up and there's nowhere to turn around."

I looked at the washed-out gullies that had once been a road, then I closed my eyes and prayed. *Dear God, take me away from here. Away from this mountain and away from this man.* But even as I prayed, I had to face the fact that no one knew where we were. No one in their right mind would brave this road, and hardly anyone used the road we'd driven on to come up here, no matter how many blackberries grew beside it. It could be days before we were discovered.

I closed my eyes again. *Please, God,* I whispered. *Help us find a way out of this mess.*

When I opened my eyes, my gaze fell upon a flat rock about 12 inches across. I bent down and picked it up. "Let's try putting this under the wheel," I said.

Chuck nodded. "That might work if I can get the left wheels over to the side of the road and keep the right wheels in the center of the old roadbed. Do you think you can fill the ruts in with brush and rocks while I steer the truck?"

I nodded and placed the rock in the truck's path. "I'll see what else I can find."

He steered the right wheel onto the rock and, gaining traction, moved the truck a bit. I surveyed the road ahead, filled with ruts, and began gathering rocks and sticks for the right wheels to roll over.

Was this task impossible? I wondered. Then I remembered all the times God had helped people overcome seemingly impossible obstacles.

> **For the Lord GOD does nothing without revealing his secret to his servants the prophets.**
>
> **—AMOS 3:7 (ESV)**

Daniel in the lions' den. Jonah inside the big fish. Jesus's disciples on the stormy sea. With every hole I filled in, I knew God was helping me. My white pants didn't matter. My cute sandals didn't matter. My overwhelming thirst didn't matter.

A peace settled over me as I worked. It was as if God's hand directed me to every rock and stick. He was helping me because I was helping myself.

It took more than 2 hours, but with me filling in holes and Chuck expertly steering the truck, we made it down the mountain. When we finally reached the paved highway, we laughed and hugged each other.

"Sorry we missed lunch," he said sheepishly, "but I'd love to take you to dinner. Somewhere nice to celebrate?"

"I'd like that," I said, as we pulled out onto the road and headed home. Chuck reached across the seat to take my hand.

It was scratched and dirty and every fingernail was broken, but he raised it to his lips and kissed it.

We didn't have many blackberries to show for our day's adventure, but God had shown us we could overcome anything if we worked together. We could even conquer Windrock Mountain.

Unexpected Redemption

Kendra Roehl

I felt angry with God, but I didn't want to admit it, even to myself. My throat was tight with emotion, and I tried to swallow the lump there as my husband, my daughter, and I drove down the road. Unwilling to let tears fall, I stared out the window as we passed bare fields with pockets of snow swirling in the winter wind. *This wasn't the way things were supposed to go. Where's the redemption in this?* I thought.

We were on our way to a funeral of a woman I'd never met, whose family we did not know. It had been several years since our adopted daughter, Jasmine, came to live with us at just 3 months old. During that time, I'd harbored dreams of one day meeting her birth parents, hoping to have a connection and relationship with them. I'd imagined what it'd be like, believing that God would somehow redeem the situation.

It had seemed my dream was about to come true when, just a month earlier, we connected with Jasmine's birth mom, inviting her to our house for Christmas. She agreed, but the day came and went without a visit. Unsure what to do, we tried without success to contact her.

We found out a few weeks later that she had been in the hospital and then passed away. All my hopes were dashed, along with the dreams I'd had of forging a connection that I believed for so long God would make happen.

As we parked at the church and got our young daughter out of the car, I was nervous. *What would this family think of us*? My husband, seeing my distress, took my hand as we walked together.

"It'll be all right," he whispered.

As we entered the large foyer, we saw many people standing around, conversing in hushed tones. The space was filled with pictures and paintings of Jasmine's birth mom. We scanned the room as a young woman approached us, smiling.

"Hi," she said. "I'm Aunt Haddie. Is this Jasmine?" We shook hands before she bent down to greet Jasmine and two more women came to greet us. One was Jasmine's grandma and the other her aunt Mary.

We made introductions and small talk before the pastor invited us into the sanctuary. As we found seats and the service started, tears began to fall as I listened to stories of a woman I'd never had the opportunity to meet but felt a connection to because I loved her daughter so much.

A knowing look passed between my husband, Kyle, and me as both aunts got up to sing, including a song one of them had written. Later we would tell them that Jasmine loved to sing and make up songs, and now we knew where she got her talent from.

As the service concluded, the people from the church smiled at us, introducing themselves. They told us they knew who Jasmine was and had been praying for her. We had no idea that we'd walked into a community of faith who had known Jasmine's mom and family for years, that they'd been raised in this community of people who had loved them well and prayed them through trials.

We were invited to stay for lunch to spend more time with Jasmine's family. As we gathered around tables, we shared about

Jasmine's life. They nodded as we talked about her interest in dance and music, her love of people and animals, her tender heart, and her sensitive spirit. They talked about her birth mom having many of the same qualities.

The hours passed too quickly and, as we were getting ready to leave, Jasmine's aunt Mary and I watched her little boy play with Jasmine. We smiled at each other in silence, taking in the moment before she said, "Isn't it amazing how God redeemed my sister's life?"

"What?" I whispered, emotion once again clawing at my throat.

She turned to look at me. "Through Jasmine," she said with a grin as I nodded in agreement.

Mary had the eyes to see how God was working behind the scenes in the very same situation I had been so angry about—thinking God had let me down. She saw God's redemption through all of it.

> Because of the LORD's great love we are not consumed, for his compassions never fail. They are new every morning; great is your faithfulness. I say to myself, "The LORD is my portion; therefore I will wait for him."
>
> —LAMENTATIONS 3:22–24 (NIV)

As we got up to leave, we embraced, with promises to stay in touch. Over the next several months, we exchanged messages and emails—Mary going into much more detail about their upbringing and Jasmine's birth mom's life, her joys and hardships. I began to understand where my daughter came from and the bravery of a woman who wanted to give birth to Jasmine even as she struggled to overcome her own demons.

Mary told me how they had prayed for Jasmine during her sister's pregnancy, and how she'd been at the birth—there to welcome Jasmine, this perfect, beautiful newborn. She told me how much Jasmine's birth mom loved her and had wanted to care for her, but her addiction and mental health made it very hard.

I described how Jasmine came to us at 3 months old. She was well taken care of, and we could tell she'd been loved. Her laid-back personality made taking care of her a joy. She laughed easily and, even as a toddler, demonstrated a sixth sense about people who were hurting and offered comfort to them.

Our conversation then turned to getting together again. With all of us in different states, we wondered when would be a good time to meet. That's when Jasmine's aunt Haddie, a missionary to Honduras, told us she and her new husband would be having a stateside reception in Oklahoma. Her sister Mary, along with several other family members, would be attending. Would we want to go? she wondered. After praying about it, my husband and I decided that our older daughter Amanda would accompany Jasmine and me from Minnesota for the long weekend of festivities.

We arrived in Tulsa on a Thursday evening after driving more than 700 miles. After greeting Haddie and Mary, Mary's husband, Thomas, and their children, Trae and Harper, in the hotel lobby, we decided to go to a local restaurant for dinner. As we sat and visited, talked about life, and acquainted ourselves even more with one another, time seemed to stop.

It wasn't until a worker kindly came and told us they needed to close the restaurant that we realized everyone else had left and it was late. We went back to the hotel and sat in the lobby to visit for a while longer until the kids got too tired. We made plans to swim the next morning and, as we got off the elevator to go to our room, I was excited about what the weekend might hold. I didn't realize the profound effect that weekend would have not only on my daughter Jasmine but on me as well.

As Friday morning dawned, we took to the pool and continued conversations about growing up, family vacations, college years, marriage, and everything else we could think of. Jasmine played with her cousin Trae and listened to him tell stories of his life in North Carolina.

We spent the afternoon at a local aquarium and the evening at another local restaurant, laughed at Thomas's jokes, and shared more stories, gaining a greater understanding of one another. There were hard stories told, mixed in with the good—honest stories best left between our hearts.

> **These commandments that I give you today are to be on your hearts. Impress them on your children. Talk about them when you sit at home and when you walk along the road, when you lie down and when you get up.**
>
> **—DEUTERONOMY 6:6–7 (NIV)**

On Saturday morning, we got ready for brunch with additional family in town for the festivities that would happen that night. Jasmine was exuberantly welcomed into this extended family with hugs and kisses while pictures were taken and presents were given.

As we left, we made plans to get ready for the wedding reception together. Amanda, as our self-proclaimed stylist, had agreed to create hairstyles for all of us, including Mary and Haddie. We met in a private room at the reception hall where Amanda worked a braid into each of our hairstyles, a similarity and a way to show our togetherness among the different styles, a unity that had developed over the past few days. As we helped Haddie into her wedding dress and oohed and aahed over the pretty bride, Mary applied makeup while Jasmine watched from the bed in the new cream dress her aunt had bought for her to wear. And it was while I was sitting there that I realized: *This is what families do. This is how they interact.*

I wondered, *How did I get to this place?* Even though I wasn't quite sure, I felt so grateful to be there. As I watched my daughter's face light up with laughter, I knew beyond any shadow of a doubt that this was where we were supposed to be.

The next day, we woke early to make the long drive back home to Minnesota. The air was filled with warm hugs and promises to get together again soon. I couldn't stop smiling as I called my husband and told him about our weekend.

Several years have now passed since that first wedding weekend together, and we continue to spend time together as a family. We've celebrated holidays and birthdays, and even

> # Whoever pursues righteousness and love finds life, prosperity and honor.
>
> —PROVERBS 21:21 (NIV)

GOD'S GIFT OF TOUCH
— Buck Storm —

HUMAN TOUCH IS a powerful thing.

Soul communicating with soul. A transfer of energy and emotion. For reasons of His own, God created us with the amazing ability to *feel*. An anxious child stills on his mother's lap, her fingers stroking his hair. A flush-faced bride after a wedding day kiss. Even the symbolic act of shaking hands transfers a skin-to-skin message of confidence and trust.

Jesus modeled touch when He used His hands to heal. The ability to touch others in godly ways is a gift from God. I can't wait to feel what it will be like to fall into the arms of my heavenly Father.

though we don't live near one another, we often have video calls and life updates.

Even though this wasn't what I had asked or even prayed for, God has a way of using what has been hard—the things that have caused us grief—to draw us to Him and to one another. It's as if redemption comes not just through His grace, but also through the people He chooses to bring to us.

The Cleft of the Rock

Roberta Messner

What has happened to Pat and me? I agonized that May morning.
I thought back to the October before when I'd visited the
antiques mall where Pat worked. I could always count on her to
be there on Thursdays—my day off and "our" day—and I was
delighted to see her. We always swapped stories about life on
the antiquing trail, sometimes laughing until our sides ached.

As I entered the shop that day, Pat's voice called out from
behind the glass counter. "I've been saving back something for
you, Roberta! A guy brought it in this morning."

Pat retrieved a finely crafted man's belt buckle from her
purse. Wrapped in tissue, it was made of tooled sterling silver
with mint-condition turquoise stones. The piece was signed by
the artist too.

"From the 1940s, wouldn't you say?" I asked.

Pat nodded with a knowing smile. "Native American.
Navajo, I'm sure." Pat was the expert on these things. She'd
checked out the artist on the computer. He hailed from
Arizona.

This was precisely the kind of piece I looked for to design
my one-of-a-kind pendants. It showed well but wasn't overly
heavy. I was already imagining it hanging from a long strand
of antique sterling beads when Pat quoted an alarmingly
low price.

"I'll take it!" I said, then hesitated. "But wait—don't you want to keep it? You love that old turquoise yourself." My eyes took in the vintage turquoise-and-silver rings she always wore, one on each finger. I smiled at her and added, "That's way too low a price."

"But you do such pretty things with these old buckles," she countered. "Besides, I bought it right."

Such was our friendship. The two of us looked out for each other. I'd styled Pat's home for a décor magazine, found treasures for her she might resell for a tidy profit, stopped by the bookstore for a new design publication she might enjoy.

But a few months ago, I'd noticed a change that made me uneasy. I still frequented her antiques mall on Thursdays, but we barely said anything to each other anymore. She never smiled. At first I chalked it up to the downturn of the antiques market. Things just weren't selling like they used to. Then Pat's hearing had gotten worse, which isolated her from people. Maybe that was it.

> When my glory passes by, I will put you in a cleft in the rock and cover you with my hand until I have passed by.
>
> —EXODUS 33:22 (NIV)

Yet when I'd steal a glance at her, she had the longing look of a little girl with her nose pressed to the window of a doll shop.

An image came to mind of me entering the antiques mall a few months before, sometime after she showed me the turquoise belt buckle. I'd been admiring some old stoneware crocks when a friend walked in and asked me about the mouth surgery I was facing. It hurt to talk so I'd whispered the details to her.

That was it! Pat couldn't hear me, and she'd misunderstood the reason for my whispering. She thought I'd deliberately left her out of the conversation.

That evening I prayed about it. "Something's wrong with our friendship, Lord. It's broken beyond repair, and I don't know how to fix it. Please help us."

The following Thursday morning I was still fretting over things when I parked in front of the mall window. Pat was there folding vintage quilts. I noticed a beautiful bow-tie design and was dying to look it over. But that meant Pat would have to help me.

I smiled as I pushed open the door. "Oh, Pat, these quilts are gorgeous," I said with as much enthusiasm as I could muster. She didn't even look up. Nervously, I fingered the bow tie. As I did my hand accidentally brushed hers. When I repeated my words, this time louder, Pat nodded matter-of-factly.

"It was made in the 1930s out of feed sacks," she said. "Pristine condition."

Pat helped me eyeball the quilt. When we turned it over for a look at the backing, I noticed something missing on her wrist. "Where's your bracelet?" I asked. Her prized starburst turquoise one.

"In my purse," she said. "I lost the stone this morning at a garage sale on Jefferson Avenue. I was looking at an old lamp. When I raised my arm, I caught it on my jacket cuff. I'm sure it fell off then."

"Did you go back and search for it?"

"Can't," she said, frowning. "I have to work. It'll be dark before I can drive there. By that time someone else will have claimed it."

"Then *I'll* go have a look," I said. My words flew out of my mouth like I'd found a bargain and couldn't wait to show Pat. "If it's not in that garage, I'll try the alley."

"How do you even know where it is?" she asked.

"I was there a half hour ago. I grew up in that neighbor-hood, Pat. Walked that alley every day of my childhood coming home from school."

I hurried to the 500 block of Jefferson in search of her stone. Combed all the familiar hiding places. Behind the for-sythia bush at the Sims's brick Tudor. Between the trash cans at the apartment building. The dip in the alley where branches liked to gather. As I canvassed the long alley, I thought of the beloved church I attended way back when. Seventh Avenue Baptist. This was the same path I took to Sunday school, Sun-day night service, Wednesday prayer meeting.

> **Finally, all of you, be like-minded, be sympathetic, love one another, be compassionate and humble.**
>
> —1 PETER 3:8 (NIV)

I heard an arpeggio from the baby grand as surely as I was sitting on the third row, piano side. The congregation sang the soul-stirring hymn writ-ten by Fanny Crosby in 1890. Those words had always been a kind of prayer:

A wonderful Savior is Jesus my Lord,
A wonderful Savior to me;
He hideth my soul in the cleft of the rock,
Where rivers of pleasure I see.

I couldn't help myself. I hummed the melody as I plodded along. It was then I heard a harmonizing hum, like a friendship sheltered in the rock the song spoke of. My voice blending with the new folks who'd moved into the yellow brick house.

If only Pat and I could be like that again, Lord. If I could just find that stone.

Despite my best efforts, absolutely nothing turned up. When I called to give her an update, I heard myself say, "God knows where it is, and I've asked Him to watch over it, Pat. When we find it—and I just know we will—I'll take it to my jeweler friend. He'll fix it so it'll never fall off again."

Do everything in love.

—1 CORINTHIANS 16:14 (NIV)

The next morning Pat telephoned. Something wonderful had happened; I could hear the old thrill in her voice. My prayer had been answered, but not in the way I'd expected. God had taken me literally instead.

"You won't believe this, Roberta," she said. "It was tucked inside the crevice of a rock. Protected in the path our cars always take."

I took Pat's bracelet and the newfound stone to the jeweler, who leaded the beautiful turquoise to the sterling in three places. "Wild horses couldn't pull it off now," he said. "It's stronger than ever."

Like the friendship I'd asked God to mend. As I headed to my car, I was back at the Sunday night gospel sing-alongs at the church of my childhood. A holy hymn filled the air. The voice was mine! The couple sipping coffee outside the Village Roaster gave me a long, curious look. Then wonder of wonders, the two of them joined in. A man in front of the Keith Albee Performing Arts Center added his baritone, completing the chorus of believers on Huntington's downtown Fourth Avenue:

> He hideth my soul in the cleft of the rock,
> That shadows a dry, thirsty land;
> He hideth my life in the depths of His love,
> And covers me there with His hand,
> And covers me there with His hand.

It seemed like the whole world was singing. Was that Pat I heard from her post at the antiques mall? Pat, who would soon be reunited with her beautiful starburst turquoise bracelet? The beloved congregation from Seventh Avenue Baptist, now scattered to and fro? Fanny Crosby's voice blending with the millions on high? Fanny, blind from 6 weeks of age, who gave us words like these because her earthly vision helped her to see what I couldn't?

I breathed a prayer of thanks for the gift of Fanny, who'd pointed me to the hidden hand of God. The One who shelters the souls of friends as surely as He does a precious stone. Covers them with His hand for safekeeping. The hand who'd guided *Roberta,* who was certain she knew all the hiding places.

Roberta, who'd missed the most important one of all. The cleft of the Rock.

Blessings in the Wilderness

Carla Gasser

I was a reasonably healthy kid until my senior year of high school, when I contracted mononucleosis twice and almost did not graduate. Gradually, I regained my strength and was able to attend college, get married, start a career, and have a family. All the things I longed for and planned to do.

But I was never the same physically. I struggled with numerous infections and chronic fatigue throughout college and my years as a high school teacher. I suffered a physical collapse and loss of strength in my arms and legs after delivering my first child and continued to deal with one health issue after another.

At the urging of my husband, family, and friends, I visited a few doctors who diagnosed me with nebulous-sounding conditions, which I completely disregarded. Ignoring the evidence of my weak, fragile, and frail body, I concluded that maybe it was all in my head. If I could only deepen my faith, pray more, and focus on God, I could overcome my physical challenges.

Since childhood, my faith in God had been the anchor that kept me grounded during times of doubt and distress. God had been good and faithful to me, and I continued to claim Psalm 16:5–6 (NIV) as my life verse, knowing that He had made "my lot secure" and had given me "a delightful inheritance."

Yet the Lord still had to teach me how to walk by faith and not by sight, and He used my health issues to show me that it was not about proving how strong my faith was but instead about acknowledging my weaknesses and putting my trust in God alone.

God got my attention when a severe stomach virus went through all four of my kids and sent me to the ER. The threat of not being there for my children was enough motivation to admit that something was wrong and to seek medical help. After 2 years of numerous tests ranging from multiple sclerosis to rheumatoid arthritis, I was finally diagnosed with systemic lupus erythematosus (SLE) by the top rheumatologist in my city.

> **Forget the former things; do not dwell on the past. See, I am doing a new thing! Now it springs up; do you not perceive it? I am making a way in the wilderness and streams in the wasteland.**
>
> **—ISAIAH 43:18–19 (NIV)**

While the diagnosis explained many of my symptoms, it did not take them away. I learned that lupus is an autoimmune disease with periods of flare-ups and remission but with no known cure.

As a busy mom of four, I did not have time to throw myself a pity party, so I hiked up my big-girl pants and put a smile on my face, masking my symptoms with a positive attitude (and a lot of makeup!).

I dealt with the infections, fatigue, inflammation, kidney, liver, and lung issues and managed pretty well . . . until I didn't.

It began with an episode of vertigo that lasted for hours and sent me to the ER. Vertigo led to other troubling symptoms: double vision, dizziness, and extreme voluntary muscle weakness. Within three months, I lost the ability to walk without help, talk without losing my voice, and see without getting dizzy.

My doctors were puzzled, my family and friends were scared, and I quickly lost hope. At my lowest point, I remember collapsing in an aisle at Target, frantically gripping the cart, and calling out to an employee nearby for help.

As I entered this deep valley, I knew I had a choice. Would I forget everything God had taught me in the light because now it was dark? Was He still a good and faithful God even in this place of pain and uncertainty? Was I only willing to follow the Shepherd down sunshine-filled paths, still waters, and green pastures? Would I trust Him to guide me even in the valley of the shadow of death?

To many who have walked their faith journey for a while, the term "wilderness experience" is familiar. The Bible uses the imagery of a desert or wilderness both literally and figuratively to describe times when God feels distant, absent, or unresponsive.

It is a place that can bring about a crisis of faith. Due to some physical, emotional, relational, or financial trauma, you feel alone, lost, and vulnerable. You may question God and isolate yourself from others.

While my wilderness journey began with physical challenges, I soon realized that my time in the desert would involve much more than my body. Yes, God took me to a dark and lonely place *physically*. Still, *emotionally* I struggled with anxiety and depression. *Relationally,* I felt lonely and misunderstood, and *spiritually*, I began to question God.

After several months of visiting specialists and running endless tests, a neurologist diagnosed me with another autoimmune disease called myasthenia gravis (MG). I had never heard of it, but my antibodies testing returned so high, the doctors marveled that I was not already in a wheelchair.

MG is a neurological autoimmune disease in which antibodies destroy the communication between nerves and muscles, resulting in weakness and rapid fatigue of voluntary muscles, especially those that control the eyes, mouth, throat, and limbs.

Just like my diagnosis with lupus, knowing I had MG helped me understand my symptoms, but once again, I faced a chronic disease with no known cure.

My heart and soul cried, "Anywhere but there, Lord." But God took my hand (and never let go) and led me through the valley. Robert Frost wrote that "The only way out is through." And it was only in walking *through* the wilderness, with God by my side, that I could see the streams of water He was providing in the desert wasteland.

> **Even when I must walk through the darkest valley, I fear no danger, for you are with me; your rod and your staff reassure me.**
>
> —PSALM 23:4 (NET)

Although they continue to play a significant role in my faith journey, my daily physical struggles are only minor detours and roadblocks. While they have contributed to the pain, doubt, and discouragement in my life, they have also brought some of the most unexpected blessings, reminding me that God still provides streams of water in desert wastelands. Grace, growth, and gratitude were three of the most unexpected blessings God gave me on my wilderness journey.

Grace: The sufficiency of God's grace is one of the most important lessons God taught me in the valley. In 2 Corinthians 12:9 (NIV), God reminds us, "My grace is sufficient for you, for my power is made perfect in weakness." At my lowest, weakest points, God's grace has sustained me. In the valley of despair, when I barely have enough light to take the next step, faith is the confidence and assurance that God knows the way, and grace trusts He will lead me safely to the other side.

> **The LORD nurses them when they are sick and restores them to health.**
>
> —PSALM 41:3 (NLT)

Growth: Although growth is often a painful process, I am thankful that I am not the same person I was when I entered the wilderness. And that is a blessing in disguise. With God's help, I did not let my painful journey break me or make me bitter. God taught me lessons I could learn no other way, and by leaning into Him, I grew tremendously. I also developed an empathy for others who are suffering, which allowed me opportunities to speak comfort and encouragement to them on their painful journeys. I continue to learn that God does not waste a thing. God comforts me so I can comfort others (2 Corinthians 1:4).

Gratitude: I now can say this with genuine conviction: The wilderness has been an unexpected gift and blessing. Not one that I asked for or wanted, but one that I needed. God used my wasteland to restore and renew me physically, to teach and

GOD'S GIFT OF SIGHT
— Lynne Hartke —

A NEW MOON marks the beginning of a lunar cycle when the moon is positioned between earth and the sun. New moon nights are dark, and for this reason, the best time to go stargazing is during a new moon. Even faint stars can be seen, resulting in thousands of stars being visible to the human eye, some reports citing around six thousand! The wisdom of our Heavenly Father understood the need for more than one light source in times of darkness.

train me mentally and emotionally, and to protect and prepare me spiritually. Only when God stripped away from me every-thing but Christ alone did I realize that He was the only gift I truly needed, filling me with gratitude. My painful journey also showed me that God uses people to support and strengthen us. People who know how to show up, when to offer words of encouragement, when just to be present, and how to stand in the gap with prayer and practical help. Words cannot adequately express my gratitude for these people.

Four years after major surgery to remove my thymus gland and stop the progression of my MG symptoms, I now can walk without a cane (and even exercise again) and carry out my daily activities without much help. I also have fewer episodes of double vision, dizziness, and muscle collapse. Some days present more challenges than others, but I have learned to respect my limitations and ask for help when needed.

Living with two chronic autoimmune diseases means that wilderness journeys will continue to be part of my life. But I have been in the dry wasteland before, so I know I can trust God to provide streams in the desert as He leads me safely to the other side with grace, growth, and gratitude.

Stuck on the Interstate

Jennie Ivey

When it comes to air travel, I'm one of those people who doesn't like to cut it close. From my home in middle Tennessee, it's an 80-mile drive to the Nashville airport. The route is Interstate 40, one of the busiest highways in the nation and one that sees more than its share of traffic accidents. Even when there are no wrecks, road construction and repair are constants.

That's why I felt so frustrated that my daughter Meg was lollygagging around my house on a sunny summer morning when she should have been packing and loading her things into my car for her flight back to Denver. Instead, she was sipping coffee and touching up her toenail polish and messing with her phone. She'd made a quick trip to Tennessee, leaving her husband and two young children behind, to attend the funeral of a friend's father.

"We should have left 20 minutes ago," I told her, trying not to let my frustration show. "Why are you just sitting there playing with your phone?"

Meg looked across the room at me and I'm pretty sure she was trying not to roll her eyes. "Mama," she said, "I'm 38 years old. I've flown thousands and thousands of miles. There's no need to get in such a tizzy. And I'm not playing with my phone. I'm monitoring the traffic app for I-40. It looks like smooth sailing."

Tizzy? Should this be called a tizzy just because I wanted to be on time? Surely Meg understood that even if the drive to the airport was uneventful, there could be significant slowdowns at security or in getting to the gate. And she needed to be there in time to fill her water bottle and visit the restroom, right? I bit my tongue rather than remind her of those things. If she wanted to be one of those people forced to dash through airports knocking people out of the way like in those old rent-a-car commercials, there was clearly nothing I could do about it.

> # The mouth speaks what the heart is full of.
>
> —MATTHEW 12:34 (NIV)

She pointed out that we were dropping her off curbside. That she wasn't checking a bag. That she'd eaten breakfast and had snacks in her purse. Most of all, she told me with a smile, she was traveling without children. Easy-peasy.

Half an hour after I thought we should have departed, Meg was finally ready to go. "How about if I drive?" she said, holding out her hand for my car key. "I'm not afraid to push the speed limit."

I gladly handed over the key. Driving on the interstate was one of my least favorite things to do. And for the first part of our trip, Meg's prediction of smooth sailing held true. There was more traffic than I would have wished, but we had no trouble maintaining a 70-mile-per-hour pace. Sometimes faster. We didn't talk much because she was too busy changing lanes and complaining about other drivers. I gripped the grab handle above my window and tried to stay calm.

Then, about 30 miles from the airport exit, things began to slow. Meg tapped the traffic app and handed her phone to me. "What does it say?"

I saw the red warning line immediately. "Looks like a wreck 10 miles ahead," I said. "Slowdowns expected."

Meg smacked a fist against the steering wheel and sighed. "Hopefully they'll have one lane open," she said. "At least we're still moving." But in just a couple of minutes, that was no longer true. All three lanes of westbound traffic came to a complete standstill. Meg opened the app again.

"An eighteen-wheeler has jackknifed," she told me. "And my flight begins boarding in 45 minutes."

I could have told her we should have left earlier. I could have asked why she spent all morning piddling around. I could have reminded her that when you're driving on a busy interstate highway, stuff happens. But I didn't say any of those things. Instead, I closed my eyes and whispered a prayer: *Heavenly Father, wrap Your healing arms around anyone who may be injured in this accident.* Then I added another plea. Compared to a truck wreck, it seemed trivial, but I added it anyway: *And please, God, let us get to the airport in time.*

I looked over at Meg, her shoulders tense, her hands white-knuckled on the steering wheel.

"There's not a thing we can do to change this, you know?" I said. She sighed and nodded. "Maybe you should take some deep cleansing breaths." She sighed again, more deeply this time, and I tried not to laugh out loud.

"I have an idea," I told her. "Instead of being upset, let's count our blessings, just like we used to do when you were little. You go first."

I expected her to say no, but she didn't. "There will be other flights from Nashville to Denver today," she said, turning her head to smile at me. "Your turn."

"We weren't in the wreck," I said, and again I sent up a silent prayer that no one was hurt.

"I have granola bars in case we get hungry," Meg said.

"It's not raining," I said.

"Or snowing," she added. (Perfect response from someone who lives in Colorado.)

"We have plenty of gas in the tank," I said.

> I love the LORD, for he heard my voice; he heard my cry for mercy. Because he turned his ear to me, I will call on him as long as I live.
>
> —PSALM 116:1–2 (NIV)

"Even though I had three cups of coffee, I don't need to use the bathroom," she said.

"Don't speak too soon," I replied, and we both laughed.

And so it went for several minutes. The conversation turned to other topics. Books we'd read. New recipes we'd tried. Podcasts we enjoyed. Our favorite strategy for solving Wordle. Then it took a more serious turn.

"Sometimes I think I'm a lousy wife and mother," Meg blurted out, and I saw tears well up in her eyes.

I pulled a wad of fast food napkins from the car console and handed them to her. "Oh, sweetie, why in the world would you think that?"

She told me how exhausted she was most days. How hard it was juggling a full-time job and taking care of her family. How impatient she sometimes was with her husband and kids. How guilty she felt being glad to come to a funeral just so she could get a break from her real life. For a long time, I listened as Meg unloaded her woes. Then I reached over and hugged her tight.

"There's not a wife or mother on earth who doesn't have those struggles or who doesn't think the same things you're thinking," I assured her. "Sometimes all you can do is pray for patience. Meet the challenges one at a time. And be grateful when you get stuck in traffic with the mama who loves you."

She dabbed at her eyes and smiled. "I am," she said. "I really am, Mama."

Finally, the traffic slowly began to move. I pulled up the airline schedule on the phone and discovered that, wonder of wonders, Meg's flight had been delayed. We would make it to the airport with time to spare. She wouldn't have to knock other passengers out of the way as she dashed to her gate. And she would, thank goodness, even have time to visit the restroom.

> **Be completely humble and gentle; be patient, bearing with one another in love.**
>
> **—EPHESIANS 4:2 (NIV)**

I found out later that though the jackknifed truck had turned over on its side and blocked all three lanes, no other vehicles were involved and the driver was okay. *Thank You, God*, I whispered. *And thank You that Meg didn't miss her plane.* Then I added a prayer of thanks for something I hadn't even asked for: the chance to have an unhurried heart-to-heart conversation with my precious daughter.

A Quirky Caveat

B. J. Taylor

"Come work with me," my husband said one Saturday morning.

"Like what? Just for today?" I asked.

"No, quit your job and work with me full time."

"Are you crazy?" I replied.

"I have to let the office girls go. We can't afford the over-head," Roger told me. "You can do the job so much better anyway."

Roger had started his own business selling tools. I knew things weren't great, but I didn't think it was this bad.

"Marriage and working together don't mix," I volleyed back. "I haven't heard of very many marriages that survive when the couple is together 24/7."

"But I need you there."

"That doesn't mean it would be good for us. What about our relationship?"

"We could make it work," Roger added.

"Let me think about it." I ran upstairs. Everything about the idea was screaming NO in my head. I had a full-time job at a big company. I'd miss the camaraderie of coworkers voicing a "Good morning" or "How's your day going?" Time in the break room was a place to catch up with a cup of coffee and to share. Then there were days off, like earned vacation and national holidays.

I *knew* what would happen if Roger and I worked together. We'd be at the office 10 or 12 hours a day and bring work home on the weekends, just like he did now. I liked putting in my 8 hours and leaving the stress of work at the office.

As I brushed my hair in front of the bathroom mirror, my thoughts barreled one over the other. We'd be in each other's faces with problems and questions and financial issues. What about setting boundaries like coming home at a decent hour to have dinner? Was I crazy to even consider this? I set down the hairbrush with a slight bang. There's no way this would ever work.

We didn't talk about it for the rest of the day, but on Sunday night Roger brought it up again. "Did you think about it?" he asked.

"I did, and I still don't think it's a good idea."

The next morning I went into work and, over a cup of coffee, told a few close friends my dilemma. "You're crazy," one said. "I could never work with my husband." Another offered her advice. "Don't do it. It'll be the death of your marriage." And another said, "I can't get through a weekend without some kind of fight with my spouse."

As I walked down the hall with a coworker whose desk was just around the corner from mine, she stopped, looked me straight in the eyes, and said, "Pray about it."

I gulped. Why hadn't I thought of that? Was it because I was afraid God was going to direct me to do this, something that every part of me was rebelling against? Financially it made sense, but I couldn't shake the conviction that our marriage would be in trouble.

Back at my desk, I took a moment to close my eyes and bow my head. *Please show me what to do, God. I'm just not sure.*

When we were both home that night, I told Roger what I was thinking. "I'm worried we'll get in each other's hair. That each of us will try to change the other and our way of doing things."

"Then let's make a pact. You handle all the office stuff, and I'll handle the sales and shipping."

"That would be good . . ." I whispered, but something still nagged at me.

"I see those wheels turning in your head," Roger said.

"Our marriage is more important than work. Our relationship comes first."

> # Now faith is confidence in what we hope for and assurance about what we do not see.
>
> —HEBREWS 11:1 (NIV)

"I totally agree. I'll tell you what," he said. "At 6 months, and every 6 months after that, we'll sit down and talk. If it's not working, quit."

I smiled. "You may think I'm a real pain to work with."

Roger smiled back. "Maybe. We'll both have an out. Okay?"

"Okay," I replied. The next Monday he gave the office staff their 2-weeks notice, and I gave mine. My boss wasn't happy to see me go, but how could he argue with my reason for leaving?

My prayer had left a niggling feeling I should say yes to Roger, and though I had a strong desire to make it work, I had a load of trepidation. What benefits would I have? Would I ever get a day off? Could our marriage survive? How could any of this be a good thing?

Over time, lots of little things came to a head. Like riding in together. He liked to stay late, I liked to leave on time. Once

I started to drive myself in and left in time to make dinner most nights, I was happier.

A big difference came to light with the way he kept his office, which was directly across from my desk.

"Can you help me find something in here?" Roger called out one day.

"It's a lost cause in that office of yours," I answered back. "Things vanish in there."

"Please?" Roger added.

"Okay, I'll help, but if I find what you're looking for, you owe me a dollar."

"Deal," he replied.

> For the LORD is a God of knowledge, and by him actions are weighed.
>
> —1 SAMUEL 2:3 (ESV)

Over the years, those dollars multiplied to hundreds, but who's counting? And that escape clause every 6 months to determine if it was working? There were a few times I wrote I QUIT in big black letters on a piece of paper and flashed it at him from his office door. We smiled, then laughed, and got over what irked us at the time.

A funny thing happened as the months turned into years— I began to understand my husband much more. He was a fantastic salesman and dedicated to making the business work. Different from working with one boss in a large company of many, I now worked with my husband, who was stronger, more forceful and focused. He had to be. The success of the company rested completely on his shoulders. He was determined to make it work not only for the benefit of us, but also for those men and women we employed. It was a heavy burden.

On national holidays when no one else came to work, Roger and I reveled in the quiet. The phone barely rang, and we had a chance to talk. Together, we set short-term and long-term goals for the business. I admired his planning, which flowed into our relationship and marriage.

> **With God are wisdom and might; he has counsel and understanding.**
>
> —JOB 12:13 (ESV)

We were very different in our work styles, but that didn't mean we weren't compatible. We both had to make adjustments and accept that each of us had our own way of doing things.

Working together was rocky at first, that's for sure, but every 6 months we invoked that quirky caveat and sat down and talked. The first question we always posed was, *Is our marriage still strong and healthy?* Second question: *Did we want to continue for another 6 months?* We discovered if we nipped potential conflicts in the bud by talking them out and not letting emotions fester, we could both find balance and adjust.

Roger and I ran the business together for 25 years. It's now been 5 years since we retired, and we are still going strong in our relationship. Through all the ups and downs, working together brought us closer than I ever thought possible. God knew it all along. I'm so glad I listened.

I Love You Because

Norma Poore

A wedding, Thanksgiving, a mini-vacation, and dog sitting, oh my! Spread out over a few months, these four events would have been manageable. However, back-to-back over four consecutive weeks, life got crazy and stressful.

My daughter's wedding was simple yet classy and small. She went from little girl to bride in what felt like a moment. As she floated down the aisle, a tear of joy left its glistening mark, but so did beauty, grace, and a big smile. Precious memories rolled across my mind. And for me, life couldn't get any better than having my children and grandchildren gathered together to celebrate a new chapter in my daughter's life.

The following Monday, I was off to the store for the last-minute Thanksgiving dinner shopping. Only half the family made the holiday but that was okay since I'd spent the previous weekend with them. Loud and energetic are the best words to describe my family. With the next few weeks being busy, I welcomed a quiet holiday weekend so I could pack. My husband, David, and I were going to Savannah to visit our oldest son, Jonathan, and his girlfriend, Heather, for a couple of days.

"You and Dad are still coming, right?" Jonathan asked on the phone the night before.

"Yes, son. We'll see you tomorrow. Looking forward to seeing you two."

"Us too. Especially since we have a surprise for you. Love you. Bye." And with that, he quickly hung up.

We enjoyed our first morning in Savannah, refreshed from a good night's sleep and ready for a fun-filled day.

"Okay, son," I said. "The suspense is killing me. What's my surprise?"

"I see you're not really dead, so you'll be fine until tonight," Jonathan teased

I love surprising my family with fun things, but don't like it when the table is turned. That night, we walked in to the civic center and saw several tables with a wide variety of nutcrackers. My heart soared. With an ear-to-ear grin, I thanked Jonathan and Heather for this wonderful surprise. I've wanted to see *The Nutcracker* ballet for many years. This was a great way to kick off the Christmas season.

> **Give, and it will be given to you. A good measure, pressed down, shaken together and running over, will be poured into your lap. For with the measure you use, it will be measured to you.**
>
> —LUKE 6:38 (NIV)

"I really enjoyed our time with Jonathan and Heather. You?" I said to David on our way home.

"Yes. It's great to see Jonathan happy. Heather brings out the best in him. Very refreshing."

"Remember, I leave tomorrow to dog-sit for Michael while he and his gang go to Florida."

"You're just Miss Popular now, aren't ya?"

The next morning, I was off to my other son's house. The song "Dizzy" by Tommy Roe played in my head. A couple of days into my dog sitting gig, I came down with a cold.

"I'm okay," I said to myself. This usually happens twice a year, in summer and early winter. I'd be back on my feet in a few days. I was wrong.

Twenty-four hours later, I knew it wasn't a cold but the flu. Thankfully, I had little to do except walk the dogs a few times a day. I did all the things you're supposed to do—get rest, drink lots of fluids, and take a good dose of vitamin C—but by the end of the week I wasn't any better. David came over my last day there and helped me clean and disinfect the house. I prayed neither Michael nor his family would get sick.

A week later, the cough and fatigue were still intense, so I went to the doctor. The flu had turned into bronchitis, and I was prescribed cough syrup and antibiotics. I hoped to be well in time to make my home festive for Christmas.

"This is the worst Christmas season ever," I said to David.

"Want me to get the boxes down from the attic?"

"Thank you, but I don't have the energy to open the boxes, much less decorate," I said.

This time of year has always been fun for me. I love the cooler weather, lights, and decorations. But most of all, I love how God brought peace on earth and goodwill to men through the birth of Jesus. That is the reason I love Christmas. At the realization there'd be no Christmas for us, hope left and disappointment took its place.

"God, why? You know I love this time of year. I enjoy expressing extra love to You, my family, and others. Sharing about Jesus's birth and salvation is something I enjoy. I can't do any of those things lying here sick. Please heal me."

After I finished murmuring, I sat in silence for a while. God brought the story of Mary and Martha to mind (Luke 10:38–42), along with a good dose of conviction. Like Martha, I was worried more about the trappings of tradition and busyness than being still before Jesus. Just as I'd complained to God about my situation, Martha had complained to Jesus because the burden of all the work was on her while Mary sat at His feet. Jesus rebuked Martha for her busyness and told her Mary was doing the better thing. Ouch.

"Honey, call the kids and cancel Christmas. I don't have food, gifts, or the stamina for much of anything. Not to mention I'd feel terrible if the grandkids got sick because of me," I said.

"The kids won't care that you don't have gifts. Plus, two of them won't be here," David said.

Christmas Day arrived and so did two of our kids with their families. I was so happy I'd listened to my husband and God, but there was no hope of a "normal" holiday. All I had was the turkey cooked the night before. Despair again settled in.

Without hesitation, my two daughters-in-law got to work cooking potatoes, heating green beans, and making gravy. Before I knew it, a beautiful Christmas meal sat on the table.

> **Do not conform to the pattern of this world, but be transformed by the renewing of your mind. Then you will be able to test and approve what God's will is—his good, pleasing and perfect will.**
>
> **—ROMANS 12:2 (NIV)**

We didn't have all the extra side dishes and goodies, but I was thankful for the girls' help and God's grace that gave me the stamina to make it to dinner. My sickness didn't change, but my poor attitude did.

Once we finished eating, I looked at the adults sitting around the dining room table and the grandkids in the living room. The rest of my despair melted away. The love of God and family is what Christmas is about.

"Grandma, where's the tree and gifts?" My youngest grandchild asked.

"Sweetie, Grandma's been so sick and not able to go to the store. I'm sorry. But as soon as I feel better, we'll have a special day to celebrate and share gifts," I said, trying not to cry. This wasn't what I wanted for Christmas, but I got a newfound determination to make the most of it.

> **So we fix our eyes not on what is seen, but on what is unseen, since what is seen is temporary, but what is unseen is eternal.**
>
> **—2 CORINTHIANS 4:18 (NIV)**

"Guys," I said, "there is something you all can do for me, if you're willing. I want to play the 'I love you' game."

I explained. "Years ago, a revivalist spoke at our church. He told us it's important for children to know they're loved, not just by their parents but by their siblings as well. He suggested this activity. We've played this game many times over the years. It would mean the world to me to do this now."

I shared the rules to this activity and told Heather she didn't have to play since she was so new to the family. But she was a

GOD'S GIFT OF HEARING
— Buck Storm —

THE FIRST TIME I visited the Church of Saint Anne in East Jerusalem, I was looking for a place to duck out of the heat and away from the tourist clamor.

As soon as I stepped inside, though, I was transported back in time. The interior was spare and stunning, but it was the choir that made my experience profound. The church is a sonic wonder, boasting some of the best choral acoustics in the world.

As the choir sang, I closed my eyes and was baptized in a nearly endless echo of song. I was in that place a thousand years ago. I was there in present day too.

Do the voices of angels ever mingle with humans? I suspect they do because I experienced it that day.

---

sport and jumped right in. One by one, we told each person, individually, "I love you because _____," and filled in the blank.

Michael went first. "I love you, Jonathan, because you're not just my brother, but my best friend."

"I love you, Mama, because when my mom wasn't there for me, you were," one daughter-in-law said.

On and on we went around the table, precious gifts of love given and love received.

"I love you, Heather, because you gave me my son back," David said.

Listening to my sons, daughters-in-law, and my husband tell one another why they're loved brought a hope-filling balm to my heart. God was right, as He always is. Christmas isn't about worldly trappings, but about love. Love birthed in a manger centuries ago that continues in and through us today.

Had I not been sick, we wouldn't have felt God's presence, nor experienced His love, hope, and reconciliation as we did that Christmas. God rarely repeats His miracles, but I pray He will repeat this one soon.

Believe that your time is
in God's hand.... Life is so
wonderful when we can come
to the point of simply trusting
God—when we can believe He
has a great plan for our lives,
even when we have questions
and can't see it for ourselves.

—Joyce Meyer, writer

CHAPTER 3

Held in His Hand

Better Plans Than Mine

Cathy Bryant

Around two hundred other people sat in the waiting area with
my husband and me, all hoping we'd be hired by the retail
company opening a new store in our area. I felt hopeful in only
one sense. We had applied for multiple jobs over the past couple
of months, and this was the first one to call us in for an interview. But the sheer number of applicants was both daunting
and deflating.

Though our work experience was in ministry and education, at this point we would take whatever employment we
could get. Our decision to return to this area to be near my
ailing mother had come to fruition two months prior. But we
hadn't counted on being without work for such a long period
of time. Our savings account was quickly dwindling, and we
both needed jobs to make ends meet.

I studied those around me and noticed that many faces were
etched with hopeless resignation. An odd mixture of nerves and
compassion coursed through me. Like me, the others must have
realized from experience how difficult it was to find work in
our rural area.

Shoes clacked against the floor in the nearby hallway. Heads
turned toward the sound and all eyes riveted on the woman
who entered the room. She announced that the interviews
were about to begin and then read names from a paper she

held in her hand. One of the first names was my husband's. He stood and moved to the hallway with others whose names were called. I immediately sent a prayer heaven's way. *Lord, You know how much we need these jobs. Please help us.*

I glanced around the room once more, taking in the faces of so many who shared our predicament. They needed work, too, and many of them had probably been searching much longer than we had. I added to my prayer. *But, Lord, I know these people need jobs too. May Your will be done.*

Not long afterward, my name was also called. I took a big breath to calm my pounding pulse, then made my way down the hall, praying the whole way for God's help. I arrived at the first interview room just as the door opened. My husband exited the room with the man who had interviewed him right behind. They carried on friendly banter, and my husband introduced me as his wife.

> **But the LORD's plans stand firm forever; his intentions can never be shaken.**
>
> **—PSALM 33:11 (NLT)**

I smiled and shook the man's hand, wishing I was as outgoing as my spouse.

The man faced my husband. "Someone will be here shortly to take you around to meet with the store manager for a second interview." Next he faced me with a smile. "Come on in."

Despite my nerves, the interview went much better than expected. The man, a manager at a store in a city south of us, was all smiles. "If you lived near my store, I'd hire you both in a heartbeat. You're two of the most qualified applicants I've ever interviewed."

Relief flooded my entire being. Maybe we had a chance at getting jobs after all.

As I exited the room, I smiled at my husband, who still waited for his next interview. The door closed behind the next applicant. I leaned toward him and whispered, "I think we've both got a really good chance."

He nodded. "I think so too."

Within a few minutes, a person escorted us both to the manager interview. I waited outside while my husband went in. Butterflies danced in my stomach, and I did all I could to send them flying elsewhere, including more prayer.

A few minutes later, my husband exited with the store manager. She smiled at him and shook his hand. "I'll see you Thursday evening."

My eyes opened wide. Had he been hired? His expression held confidence.

Thank You, Lord!

Then suddenly my mind homed in on her just-spoken words. Thursday evening. That was the night of my mom's seventy-fifth birthday party. I had been planning the family celebration since we arrived 2 months earlier.

The woman invited me in, and the interview commenced. Finally she laid my application aside, repeating the words of the man who had interviewed us first. "I feel certain that we have positions for both of you. We'll have another interview and a walk-through of the new store Thursday night. It's basically just a formality."

I needed this job so badly, but Mom's seventy-fifth birthday party was a really big deal. All my siblings would be there, and I needed to attend as well. I somehow managed to find my voice.

"I'm sorry to have to tell you this, but I have a conflict on Thursday. Is there any other time available?"

She stared at me with an expression that said, *You've got to be kidding.* Her mouth closed in a tight line, and she shook her head from side to side.

I wanted her to understand. "It's my mom's seventy-fifth birthday party, and I can't miss it."

"I'm sorry. That's the only time we have available for the next part of the process. If you can't be there, I'll have to move on to the next qualified applicant."

Disappointment knotted my throat and landed with a thud in my stomach. I managed to nod, stand, and say, "I understand. Thank you."

Once back at our apartment, I went to change clothes, grateful for the opportunity to be alone.

> I am the vine; you are the branches. If you remain in me and I in you, you will bear much fruit; apart from me you can do nothing.
>
> —JOHN 15:5 (NIV)

Lord, I'm so grateful that we probably have at least one job. But we had to wait 2 months for this opportunity. How much longer can we make it financially?

Later that week, I enjoyed my mom's party and spending time with her and my siblings, while my husband went to the interview and walk-through. As expected, he was offered the job, for which we were both grateful. But in the weeks that followed, I struggled with the Lord in prayer concerning my need for a job. What was the delay? There was no way we could make it on just one income, at least not long-term.

Not long afterward, my mom sent me a link to an online post. The elementary school I attended as a child was looking for a third-grade teacher. Even though I had the credentials to teach the class, all my previous experience was in specialized music and art classes. I felt defeated before I ever set foot in the school for an interview, certain that there would be many applicants with more experience than I.

> **When I called, you answered me; you greatly emboldened me.**
>
> —PSALM 138:3 (NIV)

The day of the interview arrived. As I entered the school, a woman exited the principal's office. She looked perfect for the job. And there was no way of knowing how many others had already interviewed.

The meeting could not have gone any better. I immediately hit it off with the principal. To my complete surprise, I was offered the job that day. To say that I hit the ground running in preparation for the school year is an understatement. There were only a few short weeks until the first day of school, and I had so much to do.

Words can't fully express how much I enjoyed that year. Though the position wasn't without its challenges, I had a great group of students and helpful coworkers. As it turns out, it didn't matter that I wasn't teaching the subject matter in which I was most experienced. What truly mattered was that I was teaching kids, and they were responding.

My biggest takeaway from the entire job-finding process was that God already knew the work He had lined up for me

GOD'S GIFT OF HEARING
— Heidi Gaul —

A SHIP'S HORN blows long and low, as if saying "adieu" to those on land. But the horn's main purpose is to signal other vessels that it is preparing to move on the water. If we slow down and listen, we may hear a similar message from God: "Listen closely. I'm on the move. Make way." At those times, by whatever means He chooses to speak, God reminds us that faith is a lifelong adventure. Listen for His signal. It's time to get on board.

when I went for that first interview. Why had I been so disheartened and disappointed? In hindsight, the teaching position was my dream job, one that perfectly matched my skill set and personality. Having moved away from our grandchildren to be near my mom, the Lord knew I needed that interaction with kids. My students were the same age as my oldest grandson, so I felt right at home with them. And if all that wasn't enough, the position paid much better than the retail job.

The whole experience taught me to trust God even in the midst of disappointment, even when things didn't initially go the way I thought they should. The prayer I prayed on the day of that first interview was absolutely answered, because I prayed for His will to be done. That's exactly what happened. His plans for me are always better than those I think I want or need for myself.

Moving beyond "My Will Be Done"

Tina Savant Gibson

Moving has always played a pivotal part in my life.

I grew up as an air force brat, where temporary was as constant as breathing and home sweet home was never permanent. Still, my little-girl soul craved a place where change meant a pocket full of quarters, not another new school.

So, when my husband and I purchased our first home as newlyweds, I was convinced my childhood prayers had been answered.

Yes, there was that season between "Wow! We have a second floor!" and "Why in the world did we ever want a second floor?" when we did consider moving. A corner lot opened up on the cul-de-sac of a super-cool new neighborhood, and we were swept away. We walked over every day and prayed as we stood on the lot, thoroughly convinced God's will (and, hopefully, our wants) would be done. But when the day came to seal the deal, we felt an unexplainable nudge to let it go, both equally convinced we should stay where we were and remodel our existing place.

At that time, we had no clue what God already knew—a handful of months later, I lost my job, and most likely we would have lost that house.

It's so easy, remembering past times like this of His protection and provision, to declare unwavering trust in His will for the future, hands held high in hallelujah.

That is, until "my will be done" desires blur His blessings, and we conveniently forget what we vowed we'd always remember: His timing is perfect. His will is way better than ours.

That's exactly what happened as my husband's retirement inched closer to reality. Uninvited conversations about relocating interrupted my comfortable routine. I was fully aware that our home of 30 years had become too big for two of us. Sure, we needed to downsize. Absolutely, we should start planning for our future . . . in the future. Not on that Saturday after donuts when he surprised me with, "Hey, what are your thoughts about moving?"

> **Trust in the LORD and do good; dwell in the land and enjoy safe pasture.**
>
> —PSALM 37:3 (NIV)

Actually, it wasn't our first discussion about downsizing from colonial to condo and relocating to another state 800 miles south. We had chatted about it off and on for years. Initially, I was all in. Living at either place would be wonderful, I thought. But sometime between those first "what if" questions and now, between the seen and unseen, second thoughts took hold. The truth I wasn't willing to admit was that my trust tank was hovering on empty. The reality of that major change had me scared out of my mind.

Instead of having a heart-to-heart with my guy right then and there, I did what those of us who want control tend to do. I dug in and wrote down all the reasons why staying put was much more "sensible" than packing up. The next Saturday morning I asked if we could talk about it again.

> **Wait for the LORD; be strong and take heart and wait for the LORD.**
>
> —PSALM 27:14 (NIV)

His smile turned serious as I slowly unfolded an 8.5- by 11-inch piece of notebook paper and began listing all the reasons why we shouldn't move away. His response? Nothing. Not a word.

He simply nodded. I assumed it was a win for Team Tina.

Fortunately, it was only a delay in what would be God's divine plan for us. I discovered that what I hoped was all settled was just gearing up, for on another Saturday, he asked if we could talk one more time.

He didn't need a piece of paper to convey his thoughts. His voice was calm, and his points were valid, and when he finished, his reasons were the complete opposite of mine.

Apparently, so was his faith. He suggested that we both pray for wisdom as well as God's will.

My piddly prayer was simple and straight to the point. "If we're not supposed to move, please change his heart. If we are, please change mine. Amen. PS—I know You'll do the right thing."

Well, I didn't really pray the "PS," but my will was no surprise to God.

And during those excruciating weeks of waiting and praying, a series of unexpected events took place.

Restructuring in my husband's company prompted us to wonder whether he might actually need to retire early, something we weren't prepared for.

Amazingly, out of the blue and amid our "what are we going to do" worries, he was offered a job transfer within his company. It was quite similar to his existing position, and it would allow him to finish his career at a place he had loved working at for over 25 years.

Not only that, but this new opportunity was located in the same state we'd been praying about whether or not to move to.

The very same state.

I couldn't argue. I couldn't chalk it up to coincidence. Honestly, I couldn't even speak as I stood in awe of God's loud and clear timing.

> **Give thanks to the God of heaven. His love endures forever.**
>
> —PSALM 136:26 (NIV)

My Sovereign Heavenly Father, the One who sees what I don't, the One who loves me in spite of me, answered my prayer. It wasn't what I prayed for. It wasn't what I wanted. It was immeasurably more. I discovered that when I surrendered to my Father's will, my doubts transformed into deeper trust.

When God moves, we might as well start packing. Whether it's across the country or within our souls, He knows our struggles and holds us close. That truth may be tough to believe in our unsettled seasons or even on a random, ordinary day. He knows that too. He loves us still.

Sometimes, His timing is crystal clear. More often, it's as thick as mud. Maybe we're not supposed to solve the marvel of His mystery this side of heaven. Maybe, just maybe, we're merely supposed to trust His will be done.

So simple, so hard, so amazing, and so worth it.

When Loss Turns to Gain

Heather Spiva

I sat down on the edge of my bed and pulled on my boots, tying one and then the other. Glancing out the window, I noticed the gray wispy clouds moving across the sky, bringing in darker storm clouds behind them.

Winds of change, just like the ones that had been blowing through my life lately.

I had just experienced a series of friendship and relationship losses that left me feeling empty and alone. Three of my very good friends had all moved away within a few months of one another, and another relationship I held dear had ended unexpectedly.

I was heartbroken. I felt bamboozled. Not by them, but by God. Why would He give me such life-giving gifts, such blessings, only to take them away? My friendships were a huge contributor to living a healthy and good life. What happiness could emerge from these changes?

I need to do something else, I said to myself, standing and shaking my pant legs down over the boots I'd just laced up. I needed to find something that would keep me busy, allow me to use my skills, and bring goodness into someone else's life.

I had heard many times that the best way to take away the pain from our own lives was to help others. I wanted to believe that God could use the current series of changes in my life to bring some good. Perhaps He intended to use my losses as an impetus to find something to help someone else that would, in turn, help me. I prayed, asking God that He would guide me to the right thing to do.

One of the buildings in my neighborhood was home to a local monthly magazine I loved. A year before, I had written a few freelance articles for them. I wondered if they had any positions open. It felt like the answer to my prayers—an opportunity to use my skills that would give me something valuable to do and help the community.

After running errands and making dinner later that day, I sat down with my husband to talk about the idea. "I need to do something else," I told him. "I think I want to write for the magazine."

"Oh, is there a position open?" he asked.

"I don't know," I said, sipping my tea, "I haven't asked them yet."

He knitted his eyebrows in concern. He was confused that I was planning to work for a magazine without even finding out if they had an opening. I understood, but I was certain I needed to ask. If nothing was open, perhaps I could be put on a waiting list and work for them in the future.

> **For the Spirit God gave us does not make us timid, but gives us power, love and self-discipline.**
>
> —2 TIMOTHY 1:7 (NIV)

The next day, I emailed the editor to see if the magazine had any editorial positions open. And wouldn't you know . . . she had just run an ad seeking an assistant editor.

She told me she already had two candidates, but she agreed to schedule an interview with me as well. Because I had already envisioned myself taking a job with the magazine—just as I had been sure the position would be open even without knowing about it—I went into the interview confidently, as if she already had hired me.

I got the job.

Almost 2 years later, I am still working there. In the meantime, the editor has become a dear friend, and I have been able to help my community with my writing. If my friends hadn't moved away, if my life hadn't abruptly changed, I probably wouldn't have sought this new direction.

> **The LORD gave and the LORD has taken away; may the name of the LORD be praised.**
>
> **—JOB 1:21 (NIV)**

While it's true that everything is always changing, we don't need to fear change. When God takes away something, He always replaces it with something that is good for us. I shouldn't have been afraid that life would never be good again. I should have held on to hope, because I have God no matter what, no matter where!

He brought new people, new experiences, and new joy into my life, all because I chose to step out, work with what I had, and make the best of my situation. Yes, He took away, but He gave back in ways I never would have imagined if those losses hadn't happened . . . and He's given me so much to be grateful for.

River House Rescue

Donna Wallace

Taking in a series of centering breaths, I noticed the aroma of pine and earth and woodsmoke on the crisp air. My vantage point from the balcony of our third-floor room in River House was like being in a tree house. I watched pearly clouds through pine boughs race against the eastern sky, mimicking white caps below. The river within a stone's throw was mesmerizing, swift and tumultuous. Surely, glacial in November. I listened to its roar as it drowned out all other sound, except for the clamor inside my chest.

I'd received news that my dad had suddenly become very sick, and my husband and I had spent months planning and preparing so we could be available to my aging parents. We'd purchased a motor home and had packed up all that was familiar and stashed it at All Valley Storage in Montana. This seemed a solid plan, but then the Cummins diesel broke down, leaving us stranded hundreds of miles from our intended destination—my folks. Repair costs were mounting, and the verdict was getting worse by the day. Had we made a terrible mistake with our well-intentioned mission to assist?

The constant noise of the boisterous river didn't help how I was feeling—unsure, even afraid. I believed God was with us. I just wasn't sure that I sensed God's presence right now, in this uncertainty. Kayakers in bright red helmets bumped and swayed past, their paddles going this way and that while navigating around boulders. My breath caught when one rolled under, then bobbed back up on the rapids, frothing white.

Upstream the flow was wide and still. Here at the bend, the swift-moving current stirred up primal fear that resided in the memory of my body, a fear borne on the banks of an equally dangerous river where I'd grown up, the Las Animas, which in contrast ran high and red in Colorado. I knew then just how unfamiliar and unprepared we were with this journey stretching before us. We had the best of intentions and thought we were ready, but now we, ourselves, needed a rescue.

I shivered and came inside to crouch in front of a crackling fire, leaving the sliding door open a few inches. God's love was nearly tangible, but I felt the shame of being distracted, vulnerable, and self-absorbed. I wanted to complain and lament, but what if my prayers were too self-centered? I looked around the room. What was otherwise an idyllic setting for a romantic getaway was proving for us to be a "neither here nor there place" laced with worry. The lovely suite booked in a hurry after our motor home broke down brought little comfort. I poked at the fire in the grate and called my friend Mary.

My spiritual friend is a wonderful listener, and after I described our situation and the swirl of emotions pooling around my desolation, Mary gently suggested I tell God all about them, and in turn, listen for His response. We waited together in a moment of quiet, then she quoted from Psalm 119:147 (TLB): "Early in the morning before the sun is up, I am praying and pointing out how much I trust in you."

"Are you outside?" she asked. Mary then described her practice of pausing and noticing God's nudges in the day-to-day—God moments, she calls them—and then rewiring her brain from fear.

With my friend's encouragement, I stepped outdoors and followed a walking path that crossed a covered bridge framed by giant ponderosas and tufts of undergrowth dotted with bright yellows and copper. Here, the river was clear and smooth as it poured gently over rocks.

Still on the phone, Mary asked, "Have you considered reading this day as you would a page of the Bible—with expectation of finding God there?" I let the gushing rhythm fill my senses, and in that moment, I sensed a void but felt held and loved, too, as a divine presence filled this sanctuary of nature—and me. I felt peace as my soul calmed.

> **Stretch out your hand from on high; rescue me and deliver me from the many waters, from the hand of foreigners.**
>
> **—PSALM 144:7 (ESV)**

Daylight settled behind the mountain in an early farewell. James and I drove to explore the artsy downtown galleries, boutiques, and brewhouses and to find a bite to eat. By the time we returned to the River House and parked on the west side, the sky was obsidian black and the air knife cold.

I was eager to snuggle in close to the fire but when we entered the room and kicked off our shoes, I heard a commotion outside. Nothing alarming at first, probably just kids being rowdy on a Saturday night. I brushed my teeth and tried to ignore it. I felt full and peaceful.

That's when I heard a woman yelling. I ran over and threw open the sliding door. Above the roar of the river below I heard, "Help! Help!" then pounding on metal. "Please! Heeellllp!"

I spun back around. "Someone's in trouble!" Panic gripped my spine. James joined my search from the balcony. Our breath puffed clouds as we madly scanned the blackness from our third-floor vantage point. Was someone in the river? James was pulling on his shoes, ready to dash down the stairs and out around the building. With all my senses on high alert, I stretched my body over the railing. It was a woman's voice. I imagined her trying to escape an attacker. "Oh God, help!" I prayed.

> **I keep my eyes always on the LORD. With him at my right hand, I will not be shaken.**
>
> **—PSALM 16:8 (NIV)**

When the banging subsided, I realized it wasn't a distant voice at all, but rather a quavering, frightened crying close by. Was it from the narrow balcony directly below us? I leaned farther still and glimpsed the tops of two snowy white heads. Surely it wasn't these two making all that racket. I searched the expanse of darkness again but didn't see anyone else.

"Are you okay?" I called down to be sure.

I could see the tops of their heads turning from side to side, "No! Please help us!" In breathless phrases the woman explained to the darkness how after they arrived in their room, they'd stepped out onto the balcony only for a moment, but the security bar had fallen into locked position when they closed the sliding door behind them, and now they were stuck outside with no phone, no shoes, no coats, and no way to get down.

And no one to hear their cries for help. Their voices were not carrying over the river. With the temps falling they must have been frightened half to death that this was how their story was going to end.

"We'll ... get you ... help," I cupped my hands and hollered in their direction.

"I can't see you!" the woman cried, her head turning this way and that.

"I am up here." I addressed them at the top of my voice. "I am here!"

The man's shoulders were bent, his voice barely a murmur above the river. So capable just minutes before, they were both frail now; their trusted resources all gone missing— their money, their intellect, their area of expertise or fame, none of it mattered now. In a moment, they were entirely vulnerable. This wasn't a car crash, not a broken hip ... but they might have perished all the same.

> **I sought the LORD, and he answered me; he delivered me from all my fears.**
>
> —PSALM 34:4 (NIV)

"It will be just a moment. Here you go." I lowered a throw blanket. Gnarled hands reached up to receive it.

And then we waited, together, the pulsing of the river filling the silence.

Soon a hotel employee showed up with a flashlight and stepped into a circle of light. She surmised the couple's plight as they gestured a short repetition of their story. She raced to remedy the situation.

"Thank you," they called in unison.

GOD'S GIFT OF HEARING
— Buck Storm —

IT'S INTERESTING HOW our brains will tune out a consistent sound like the hum of an air conditioner or the purr of an engine. I think about this occasionally. My wife and I often use a fan at night, a practice we picked up over years of travel. It's funny— unless I'm thinking about the fan noise, it just disappears.

Does this mirror my spiritual life? I suspect the low drone of life sometimes (often) blocks God's whisper from my ear.

Forgive me, Lord.

I think it's time to turn off the fan and use the ears God gave me to hear His voice.

We wait for the God who comes, sometimes in the quiet and sometimes by taking bold action, yelling with all that is in us. How brave the elderly woman was, hollering with all her might over and over, even lifting a metal chair and beating it against the wrought iron railing in order to be heard above the water breaking on the rocks below. I imagine her straight out of the pages of a gospel narrative.

The couple never did see me. I wanted to take them hot tea for freezing hands and throats yelled raw, but I wasn't meant to be seen in their rescue plan. In fact, the story wasn't about me at all; instead, I was gifted with a box seat to a beautiful God moment.

God is found in the pages of Holy Scripture, in nature, and yes, in the quiet inner reaches of one's own self. Sometimes

God comes in a familiar voice or in strangers who run to meet us or rescue us.

"All will be well now," I said to the tops of their heads before going back inside. And to God I whispered, "Be pleased, O LORD, to deliver [us]; Make haste, O LORD, to help [us]" (Psalm 40:13, NASB1995). I knew in that moment my rescue was on its way too.

Making Space for Everything Lovely and True

Eryn Lynum

Sunlight rattles the door of my dreamworld—at first a respectful rapping upon my eyelids, then an abrupt and invasive knocking. Finally, my eyes creep open, and I find my three young sons already stirring in the adjacent queen-sized bed. A stretched moment passes before I can orient myself. Oh, yes . . . we are homeless. But by choice. This hotel room is our residence for the day.

I watch those three boys rustling in the covers. I smooth my hand over my belly growing with new life. *Have we really chosen this for our family?*

Yesterday we sold our home, and by today's end, we're determined to locate and purchase a used travel trailer that will serve as our home-on-wheels for the next 9 weeks. This road trip is an adventure we've dreamed of as a family for years, an opportunity to explore areas across the Pacific Northwest where my husband lived during his childhood.

My husband recently left his job to begin his own business. Now, with our home sold, we have no mortgage or employer tethering us to one place on the map. We see it as a rare opportunity for a sabbatical, to step away from the normal routines of life and focus on us as a family. Our boys, ages six, four, and two, are as eager for the adventure as we are, secure in the promise that after 9 weeks, we're coming back to Colorado to our friends and church family. My prayer is that these travels will, in a way, ground us.

We have never needed this more than now. Over the previous year, our days shifted up to an uncomfortable pace. We felt time slipping through the hourglass, sucking us straight down with it. This trip is a casting away of old habits. It is a challenge of societal norms. We need to step outside our surroundings to gain perspective and gather back only what we truly want to give space to in our lives. We need to pare back the distractions, clutter, and noise to distinguish what actually allows us to thrive.

Yet this wasn't an act of defiance against society—it was a rebellion against our own discontent. We are eagerly pursuing a life marked by the life-giving boundaries of restraint, intentionality, and living by what we value.

The majority of our belongings are gone—sold or donated. The carefully chosen remaining items are stacked in a 10-foot by 12-foot storage unit, smaller than most bedrooms. We are parting with our things. More importantly, we are distancing ourselves from our everyday routines as a family.

We need a reset of the soul.

In over 2 months, when our whirlwind trip is complete and we return home to Colorado, I pray we'll know exactly what to gather back into our new home and what to invite back into our schedule. More pressing, I ache to know what to leave out—to identify what fluff and clutter have been distracting us from God's best. In a way, this trip itself is a prayer; a laying down of our lives before God and a request for direction. We have felt unsettled, like we're trading out the abundant life God has for us for busyness. As we drove west through the mountains, my prayer was this: *Lord, teach us what it looks like to work hard and rest well; to live by our values in a way that aligns with Your best for our family.*

> I am the true vine, and my Father is the gardener. He cuts off every branch in me that bears no fruit, while every branch that does bear fruit he prunes so that it will be even more fruitful.
>
> —JOHN 15:1–2 (NIV)

In the coming weeks, we watch our boys absorbed in wonder at God's wild world. I cannot help but be sucked in myself. Brightly colored starfish keep our attention for hours. Gray whales wave to us from cerulean waters. One day, translucent moon jellies greet us from the inlet near where we've parked the trailer for the week. They're so plentiful the water is thick with them. The boys lay on their bellies, heads hanging over the water, gently touching the jellies with their fingertips.

The more time we spend here, the more I feel connected to God's natural rhythms. The tide follows the moon's lead—waters drawn out, then gathered back in each day. A purging. A cleansing. A selection.

I think about Jesus, present at creation and there at the Father's side. He took part in engineering these water systems and the expansive galaxies, and the rhyme and reason of it all. I hear Jesus's words, spoken to His followers in John 15, comparing himself to a vine and his Father to a gardener. When Jesus speaks of pruning the vine so it can bear fruit, he is not talking about their salvation. He assures them in the following verse: "You are already clean because of the word I have spoken to you." He calls them His own.

I, too, am secure. I have not come to these waters to find salvation—only to deepen my roots in the Father, to practice abiding.

As a family, we've lost our way a bit. The stress of my husband's former job has affected all of us. We were tired, overwhelmed, and had forgotten how to have fun together. Our kids are struggling with obedience, which signals to us that we're not spending quality time engaging with them. And when was the last time my husband and I went out on a date together?

Two years prior, we wrote out core values for our family, including these: "Share the gospel in our home," "Spend time in creation," and "Do life together as a family." We saw each of the values struggling beneath the weight of our overstuffed schedule.

I think we can bear more fruit, and I believe it begins with our lifestyle. I see us as that branch abiding in Christ, depending on Him for all things, yet wavering. As we hesitate to trust Him, we pine for control. I know I do. Striving to provide by my own means, I accumulate clutter. Our agenda fills with activity and work. Our home fills with things that serve little purpose and give even less joy. My branch is choked by a creeping vine of distraction and surplus.

We've come to these waters to be pruned—to heed God's reminders of what this life is for.

Living squished together as a family of five-going-on-six in a 20-foot travel trailer delivers ample lessons right to our aluminum doorstep. We're learning to live with less. Our trip-worthy items, including books, journals, hiking packs, art supplies, and minimal cooking equipment, are organized like a game of Tetris into the limited storage spaces of the trailer. Sharing is essential. Depending on neighbors at campgrounds and old friends we reconnected with along the journey is a blessing. The only luxuries are the stretching views and invaluable experiences out in nature.

> **The LORD replied, "My Presence will go with you, and I will give you rest."**
>
> —EXODUS 33:14 (NIV)

A shift takes place in the middle of our trip—much like the shifting of the seas we watch each day. My soul slows down. It changes direction. I find satisfaction in sitting, in stopping, and in delighting in the works of the Lord. Our boys shed any residual stress much quicker than my husband and I do. It takes them a couple of days on the beach, running through lapping waves on the shore and sorting shells, to remember what life is for. I watch the effects of our recently stressful days melt away from my husband; he is learning to dream again, scratching designs on paper for his carpentry work and developing an eagerness to return home and build his business in a way that aligns with our family's values.

Nine weeks later, entering back into our regular activities, we encounter essential decisions needing to be made. However, for the first time, they really look exactly like that: decisions. We get to choose what we fill our life with. Moving from a 200-square-foot travel trailer to a 1,700-square-foot rental home leaves a lot of blank space. We decide to unpack our storage unit slowly, purging our belongings of what, after 9 weeks away, we decide we no longer need. It is September when we return, and although we homeschool our kids, activities are kicking into gear. We have a new caution around what we write onto our calendar. We add in my regular fall Bible study, but other than that, we allow our agenda room to breathe and hold off on committing to too many activities. Although my husband is excited to start his business, we have essential conversations around what that means: What kind of hours should he work, and what boundaries should we set around work commitments and projects?

> **You make known to me the path of life; you will fill me with joy in your presence, with eternal pleasures at your right hand.**
>
> **—PSALM 16:11 (NIV)**

Our time in the travel trailer and away from our regular routine granted us the perspective to make hard adjustments in our life. As we slowly unpack the trailer and our storage unit, I also begin unpacking my heart of the many lessons learned on the road. As I sort out my thoughts around our trip, I hear God's answer to my prayer. He has successfully stripped away the distractions and granted us clarity. He's given us this fresh start so that we can choose His abundant life, one marked with purpose, praise, and joy.

With our spirits set to the pace of the ocean—under God's rhythmic, unhurried design—we place new value on time together as a family. We've become acutely aware of everything

GOD'S GIFT OF SIGHT
— Heidi Gaul —

GOD SEES US during times of hardship. During my battle with breast cancer, my heart was in turmoil. I needed help. More than that, I needed to know I wasn't alone. As friends and family held me close, I saw God's love reflected in their eyes and felt comforted. When we seek to comfort others through their times of suffering, may they see that same love reflected in our eyes, and God's concern in our smiles.

that pulls us apart or adds unnecessary hurry to our lives. We make counter-cultural decisions to refuse rush, to embrace God's rest.

At the ocean's edge, God was igniting a flicker in our family that would grow with time. Of course, it would ebb and flow as these things often do. At times, in the years to come, I would wonder if we'd forgotten all we learned during our trip. But then God would fan that flame, align our values to His own, and set us back on course. We cast away all that is holding us back from His abundant life and gather in everything that embodies His best for us—everything lovely, true, noble, and praiseworthy. This is what we're choosing to gather.

The Beautiful Garden of Prayer

Kathie Kania

Tangles of brush and wild grapevines almost obscured the old tractor path winding up the wooded hill, but I could still make it out. The late summer sun of rural western New York simmered up fragrances of leaves and wild berries but also caused my fifty-something body to sweat. I swatted a deer fly away as I wrestled a vine. *It's right about here . . . There's the big tulip tree; now I turn right. About twenty steps, if I remember.* Yes: There was the small, sunny opening, and I looked around with a delighted, amazed smile: I'd found the BGOP!

I was just a child when this spot in our south woods became special to me. I'd had a dream that a rocket ship had landed there from Mars and created the star moss that was abundant right in this spot and rare in other places in the woods. It was soft as a comforter; I could lie on it or sit on it, and it sprang right back up, its beautiful little bright chartreuse stars as resilient as tiny springs. Young maple trees encircled the sunny spot the way gentle hands cup a rescued butterfly, and I felt safe and unseen there. I often went to that spot to lie in the downy moss and scheme—or cry, or pray, or write dumb poems about an admired boy—while looking up at passing clouds. As an older child, I dubbed the spot "The

Beautiful Garden of Prayer," or BGOP for short, in honor of a hymn I liked.

Growing out of my teen years, I moved to nearby Erie to work at a hospital and maintain a sparse, old, third-floor apartment that I loved, but I didn't forget the BGOP. Visiting the family on weekends, I often slipped away to walk up that tractor path, turn right at the big tulip tree, and walk the twenty steps to kneel in the star moss, to pour out problems in prayer. The Lord seemed so comfortingly near in that garden of prayer! It felt good to ask Him aloud if I should switch jobs . . . or go to college (which one?) . . . or date this or that guy.

> **Every good and perfect gift is from above, coming down from the Father of the heavenly lights, who does not change like shifting shadows.**
>
> **—JAMES 1:17 (NIV)**

Then along came Brad, an exciting young man— nice-looking, bright, and daring; unpredictable, scathingly outspoken, and funny. I just knew he was for me! Eventually all my friends met him.

"I don't know." Trudy carefully tiptoed around my questions. "I have to admit that I don't care for him."

Another time, Marisue intimated quietly, "I wouldn't like it if my boyfriend spoke to me like Brad sometimes does to you . . ."

But what did they know? They hadn't spent the time with Brad that I had; they hadn't enjoyed his razor humor or admired his swaggering intelligence and vast vocabulary. I'd show them how perfect he was for me. Brad and I had some golden times—picnics on Lake Erie, trying out different restaurants, sifting through old antique shops. He would often try to "improve" me, and maybe I felt as if I needed improvement, standing next to someone so cosmopolitan. Sure, sometimes he was sarcastic, but when I objected, he was quick to reassure me that it was just a joke and that I was being overly sensitive. The good times outweighed all that. Time with Brad was never boring. That's what I wanted.

I knew from reading my Bible that if I had faith even the size of a mustard seed, the Lord would give me "the desires of [my] heart" (Luke 17:6 and Psalm 37:4, NIV). I had all the faith I needed, and the prayers I spoke in the BGOP were filled with absolute surety. I knew I wanted to spend my life with Brad. I had dated others in my young life, and nobody else measured up. I was sure I could be happy with this exciting man. I laid this all out to the Lord. I even took Brad to church with me. Although some eye-rolling took place, he did go. And he admired my love for God. Sometimes he talked about our someday-marriage. Didn't that seal it?

Up to then, my prayer garden could hardly be called a garden; it was just an open circle of sunlight about 15 feet across, with a large plush-pillow of star moss in the center. Beautiful, yes, but suddenly I was filled with an even bigger ambition: I would build a spectacular living monument to the Lord. It would be a testimony to our agreement about my spending my life with Brad.

"This is in honor of You, Lord," I said the next week as I breathlessly lugged a burlap bag and a pail of water up the hill, turning right at the tulip tree. I carefully planted a new crimson rosebush I'd bought, along with some alyssum, which would turn into a carpet of white flowers. I edged the planting design with blue lobelia seeds. It would be a gorgeous combination of color, surrounded by the rich green of the star moss, living proof of my unwavering faith. With a final prayer, I watered all the plants and seeds carefully and headed down the hill with my garden tools, a smile on my face.

Over the next many weeks, my busy schedule in Erie kept me away from the farm. Truthfully, I didn't think of the BGOP very often. But when I did, I wasn't worried. We got intermittent rain and sun that time of year, with mild temperatures. Besides, this was the Lord's garden, and it would be secure without a great deal of fussing. It was all part of my monumental faith in my future, the wonderful secret I shared with Him!

> # He has made everything beautiful in its time.
>
> —ECCLESIASTES 3:11 (NIV)

Soon, it was time I went home to see how things were going. I spent some time visiting with my parents and younger sisters, and then I slipped away up the tractor path in the golden sun of late afternoon. I walked the twenty steps and covered my eyes, smiling, so the beauty of the garden would have its maximum effect. I removed my hands.

My smile dissolved. The rose was a parched brown stick. The alyssum plants were faded, tan ghosts, lying flat. The lobelia seeds had never emerged; there was just a ragged, dirt scar. There was nothing. Only the star moss remained with its scratched-out furrows, looking defiled and pitiful. I did not pray that day. Sullen, I traipsed down the hill, not on speaking terms with the Lord.

Over the next few years, the moss healed itself and grew back in the scraped rows. I forgave the Lord, returning now and then to my BGOP. I realized that I'd been foolish to plant nursery flowers where the hard-yet-sandy, too-often-shaded soil was only habitable for moss and woodsy plants.

But more than that, I wondered if my dying garden was perhaps more of an answer than I realized. I had thought the Lord didn't care about my faith. Perhaps He cared more than I realized. Perhaps a dead stick and a scratched-out furrow was His decisive, attention-getting "No."

And hadn't He helped me when, a couple of years after planting that doomed garden, I finally made the decision to break it off with Brad? When I'd finally heard one critique too many? When I waited yet again, nicely dressed and ready, for a date to which Brad didn't show up or even call to cancel? Didn't He send unexpected peace when I sent that letter breaking things off to Brad's out-of-town apartment (a place he'd never even invited me to see)? Didn't He give me projects and other activities to keep me busy over the weeks that Brad never responded to that letter? He even brought my friends around me lovingly—friends who never said, "I told you so." These gifts all came down in loving comfort around me, and at just the right time.

> But those who hope in the LORD will renew their strength. They will soar on wings like eagles; they will run and not grow weary, they will walk and not be faint.
>
> —ISAIAH 40:31 (NIV)

Then there came a day, a few years after I broke things off with Brad, that I hurried up the tractor path to my BGOP, all out of breath. I didn't have much time, with all the plans.

"Well, I guess this is it," I said happily. "Goodbye, Prayer Garden. I don't know how soon I'll see you again. I'm getting married to a really wonderful man, and we're moving out west so he can finish graduate school." Michael was witty, intelligent, funny, smart . . . *and lovingly considerate*. I looked at the hummock of moss and smiled. "Thank You, Lord. I'm sorry I was mad about the flowers and that silly deal I tried to make with You. Thank You for not letting me force Your hand!" I hurried down the path and away to another life.

Now, 25 years after that last visit, I broke through the brushy edge of the lane, pushing a lock of graying hair away from my glasses, looking around, making sure this was the right tulip tree. The trees around it had grown! While visiting Mom and Dad, I wanted to just take a peek at that funny little spaceship landing site, that poem depot, that blessing-on-demand spot, my Beautiful Garden of Prayer where I learned that He *does* make all things beautiful in His time. *I think this is the right tulip tree.* I walked the twenty steps, wrestling vines and hoping I hadn't strayed from what used to be a footpath. But no—this was the place, all right.

No wonder it took me a moment to recognize it. I smiled tearfully. Over the pillow of moss, the Beautiful Garden of Prayer was covered with a latticework of delicate white flowers! Woods-loving wildflowers in profusion on the thin, woody stems of some vigorous sapling. A huge beautiful, living, welcoming bouquet.

Just like my life, the blooms had come in abundance when His time was just right.

GOD'S GIFT OF SIGHT
— Buck Storm —

I'M CONVINCED I miss things. It's as if my life is on cruise control. But lately I've been making a change, starting with what's visible (recent LASIK surgery has helped this!). I don't want to simply look, though. I want to *see*. And not only the natural beauty—that's easy—but the gloriously mundane. The tree in my yard isn't the same tree it was yesterday. It's a wonder, a heavenly sculpture ever changing. Dust in a sunbeam, the curve of my granddaughter's cheek . . .

Lord, give me wide-open eyes to take in everything You have for me.

I see clearly now. There is no mundane—only the *miraculous*.

The Worry Box

Roberta Messner

The clerk at my physician's office handed me my visit summary for my three-month checkup. My problem list included a new entry in bold, black type: CAD.

"There has to be some mistake," I said. "I can't have coronary artery disease. I've never had chest pain or high blood pressure or shortness of breath . . . or *anything*!"

My physician shot me a perplexed look from the hallway, then steered me into a nearby exam room. "That stands for chronic anxiety disorder, Roberta."

He couldn't be serious. Real Christians didn't have anxiety disorders. Did they? Was I really that bad?

My mind traveled back to the evening I arrived home to check on a repairman's work. He'd been there for 6 hours, but the patch on my bathroom wall was still visible. The guy wasn't even finished, and I'd already started "awfulizing."

What if he never gets it right? The semigloss paint I'd purchased would only highlight the flaw. I'd see it every time I walked into the room and get upset all over again. My palms became sweaty, and I could feel my heart pounding. *But it's okay,* I reasoned. *I can solve this problem.* I riffled through the garage until I found some old-timey beadboard I'd purchased from a salvage yard. *Best to be prepared for these things.*

Truth be told, my anxiety had become a lifelong pattern. "You've always been a worrywart," a friend once chided. I knew what-ifs dominated my life. I simply tried to address them before they got worse. If I didn't, who would? I was a woman living on my own. One with a serious chronic illness to boot. So many things seemed out of my control. Life was one big uncertainty that I tried to fix.

So naturally I attacked my anxiety. When I read up on the subject, the stories sounded all too familiar. One expert said it was like using high-powered adrenaline to swat flies. When that happens, a person's body responds as if they're in real danger. When you're on alert for every little thing, it takes a huge toll on your health.

> **Therefore do not worry about tomorrow, for tomorrow will worry about itself. Each day has enough trouble of its own.**
>
> **—MATTHEW 6:34 (NIV)**

I'd tried to live by faith and not borrow trouble. But I'd become an awfulizer of the worst variety. I only gave my problems to God after *I* tried to take care of them. When I turned things over to Him, He sometimes seemed to take His good ol' sweet time. With my palms sweating and my pulse quickening, I'd be onto another solution of my own.

My job-related anxiety was the worst. When I was at work, I thought about work, and when I was at home, I thought about work. Sometimes an irrational, almost paralyzing fear took over. Every day I put more and more pressure on myself to do things right and to ensure perfect outcomes.

One day, my boss at the VA Medical Center told me another nurse would be moving to my office. Julius was his name. People were always talking about the nurse from Nigeria with the big smile. When I'd see him around our hospital, I always marveled at the peace he exuded. Rumor had it that as he drove up our long, winding hill each morning, he paused at every American flag to pray for the patients he would care for, the families he would meet, the staff he would work with.

What would he think when he teamed up with the likes of me, when I oriented him to our office and he saw what a basket case I could be?

On Julius's first day on the job, I started with the boxes where I organized my day-to-day functions. Hospital-acquired infections. Issues affecting our satellite clinics. Referrals to local and state health departments. And on and on. At long last, we were finished. Or so I thought.

The Lord is my strength and my shield; my heart trusts in him, and he helps me. My heart leaps for joy, and with my song I praise him.

—PSALM 28:7 (NIV)

Julius pointed to a tidy, unlabeled box, its lid secured tightly with rubber bands. "This box is special!" he said, admiring the red, white, and blue hearts and American flag on top.

I ventured a sheepish smile. "Oh, that's my secret stash. My worry box. Some of it's been there for eons." I could feel my heart hammering just thinking about all the worries I'd stacked in that box.

Julius waited patiently, as if inviting me to explain. I slid off the rubber bands and lifted the lid. "When I'd done all the damage I could do, I put all the problems I couldn't solve in here. Out of sight, out of mind. Sort of. Here's one for you. An outbreak at a nursing home. I prayed and I stewed. But it got so involved, I just threw up my hands and gave it over to the box."

Julius placed his large dark hand over mine as if nudging me to see things differently. "What happened, my friend?"

"Well, I worked with the facility to relocate the patients. Got the staff on board with education. Made sure everyone received the right treatment. But I got overwhelmed. Wanted things to be perfect. All that was left was to relinquish it to the box."

"What was the final outcome?" Julius wanted to know.

I thought for a minute. Not a single patient had suffered dire consequences. The nursing home became stronger than ever in the care the staff provided. I stared at Julius in disbelief. When I put a problem in that box, I wasn't trusting God to take care of the situation. Instead, I stewed over it. The worry box had become a reminder of all the times I thought I'd failed. Now, under Julius's gentle questioning, I realized that I hadn't failed at all. And neither had God.

I pulled out another document, and another, and revisited their content. A patient who wasn't getting any better. One estranged from his out-of-town father. An email from a doctor who planned to challenge me in a meeting.

It was incredible. Not a single one of those anticipated disasters had ever come to be.

"How in this world . . ." I heard myself mutter.

Julius patted my worry box as if blessing it. "It wasn't *of this world*, Roberta," he said with that peaceful way of his. "When you did all you could and asked God for help, He did the rest. The very heavens opened up for you." Julius reached for one of the documents and let it cartwheel through the air, beaming as it fell back into the box. "Maybe this is not a worry box. I think it's a trust box."

When I arrived at work the next morning, Julius was already there, smiling that ever-present smile. Front and center on my desk was my newly christened trust box. On the lid, he had taped a Bible verse he'd clipped from the devotional book he kept on his desk: "Cast all your anxieties on Him because He cares for you." Julius said the word *cast* meant to hand it over, once and for all. The two of us vowed we would prayerfully place issues in its keep that we were leaving in God's care. And then we would *not* obsess over them.

> **Trust in the LORD with all your heart and lean not on your own understanding; in all your ways submit to him, and he will make your paths straight.**
>
> **—PROVERBS 3:5–6 (NIV)**

Being diagnosed with CAD, along with Julius's wisdom, changed me for good. I became more aware of my anxious tendencies and the control I tried to exert over situations that were beyond my control. Now, when the threat of anxiety tries to rear its ugly head, I stop and take a deep breath. My mind quiets as I recall all the times God has been there for me in the past. Though I sometimes am tempted to revert to my old, anxious ways, I have learned to put the situation in *God's* capable hands, trusting in *His* love and wisdom. Not mine.

God's Goodness Doesn't Stop

Angela Scully

In college my roommate used to quip that God gave me unco-operative hair to remind me I am *not* in control. The irritat-ing accuracy of this statement resonates with the truth that my default mode is attempting to control most things in my life. Over the years, I've not-so-jokingly joked that God has been teaching me the lesson of trusting Him—but I've yet to actually learn it. No matter how many times my control issues make a mess of things, I always seem to fall back into believing it's safer when I'm pulling the strings.

That's probably why when God called me to attend seminary, He made it look like it was my idea. God showed me, one step at a time, where He was leading me, knowing that if He didn't ease me into His will, I would likely panic and run the other way.

I entered college as a history major with grand plans to get my masters in Egyptology and forever spend my days catego-rizing artifacts in the basement of a museum. I decided to take Greek—which fell under our biblical literature department—because it was one of the only languages my university offered that related to my field.

As I began to learn and study the ancient language of the New Testament, I was mesmerized by how much it illuminated my understanding of the Bible. Soon I was taking multiple biblical literature courses, hungry to study more. By graduation, I was one course away from being able to declare a double major in history and biblical literature. One afternoon, as I walked to my college dorm room, the idea that "seminary might be fun" suddenly entered my mind.

And that's how God got me to go to seminary.

At the beginning of my seminary career, I volunteered for a local ministry that served women transitioning out of the sex industry. The first time I visited the transitional home I felt unqualified. I recall sitting in my car praying, "God, are you sure it's me you want to do this? My experience can't relate to theirs. What can I possibly offer them?" Exploitation, abuse, addiction—these were not part of my story. In the driveway that morning, God calmed my spirit by impressing on me that my experience as a woman was enough to connect with their stories. *"I'll do the rest."*

And that's exactly what He did. He filled in the gaps so I could fearlessly serve these women, and in turn, they ministered more deeply to my heart than I could ever imagine.

Eventually, I was hired on as a member of the weekend ministry staff. I felt I had found my passion and my calling. Nearing graduation, I needed to figure out my future. My supervisor told me there was a full-time position they wanted to create for me. I felt like everything was falling into place.

Then, just as it seemed God was laying out my future perfectly, the floor fell out from beneath me.

My ministry supervisor called with incredible news. Someone had donated a house to the ministry. *A whole house.* Amazing! This meant we could start offering space for women on the waiting list. In recovery ministries, waiting lists can be a death sentence.

And then came the bad news.

"Unfortunately, expanding the current ministry means we don't have the funds to create your position. I'm so sorry."

My heart dropped.

In the moments immediately following that phone call, I sat on the couch in my apartment feeling hollow. And so I, a newly graduated seminary student, did what any good ministry graduate does. I prayed.

But they were not holy prayers. They were bitter, blaming prayers. "God, I've done *everything* You've asked me to do, and *You dropped the ball.*"

Yup. That's actually what I said *out loud* to God.

"*You need to read Job,*" God seemed to say to my heart. I was not amused. But I begrudgingly obeyed.

I began to withdraw. From church. From my friends. I rationalized that I was being responsible only using my gas money to go to work where I actually got paid. And even still, I was making half the amount I needed to pay my bills. In addition to everything else, the people closest to me whom I could normally ask for help weren't able to help.

> Cast all your anxiety on him because he cares for you.
>
> —1 PETER 5:7 (NIV)

I was drowning. All my safety nets were cut. And it was all God's fault.

Or at least that was my perception at the time.

In the midst of all of this, my church began a series on tithing. *Not funny, God.*

I especially was not delighted when I felt God tugging on my heart to give a very specific amount as my tithe—more than the typical 10 percent.

"Okay, God, I'll tithe that amount when I'm back on my feet."

God was not playing. *"If you can't trust Me in your lack, you won't trust Me in your plenty,"* I heard loud and clear. Maybe that is what God was trying to get across when He told me to read Job.

On the floor of my bedroom, I exchanged my bitter prayers for prayers of faith in His goodness. "God, I don't feel it or see it, but I am *choosing* to believe You are still good." I prayed this over and over and over.

Not long after this, a church friend sent me an email. She let me know how much I had been missed at Life group and asked if everything was okay. Everything wasn't, but I didn't want to let her know that.

> **Jesus Christ is the same yesterday and today and forever.**
>
> —HEBREWS 13:8 (NIV)

Isolation was my default when I was struggling. After all, this was *my* problem, so naturally I was the one who needed to fix it.

But I emailed back and gave her a very generic overview of what had been happening. I told her that because of this blow to *my* plans, I didn't feel I could afford to drive in one direction for church on Sundays and the opposite direction for work Sunday nights. She responded quickly and offered her condolences for my lonely struggles. She followed up with, "I know you feel you can't afford to, but will you trust me and come meet me for service tomorrow?"

I told her I would, but I secretly planned to "accidentally" sleep through my alarm the next morning. My plan was thwarted the next day when my phone rang an hour before

I had to get up. It was my friend. I groaned but answered it anyway. Her voice was way too cheery for that early in the morning.

"I just wanted to make sure you were still planning on coming to church with me this morning."

We sat through service and talked some after, then she invited me over for lunch. I stayed after lunch, took a nap, and attended Life group for the first time in a few weeks. I had to work that evening so I intended on leaving early. I'll be honest, I spent a lot of our meeting time stressing about how I would get to work without running out of gas. Shortly before I had to leave, my friend pulled out an envelope and handed it to me. Our group had generously collected money for me. The amount was exactly enough for gas and groceries for the week.

> **Commit your way to the LORD; trust in him and he will do this.**
>
> —PSALM 37:5 (NIV)

But God's goodness didn't stop there.

Friends started dropping groceries and meals off at my house. Many of them had no idea what was going on. People at church started handing me gas cards, saying, "I don't know why, but God told me to give you this."

Then the most amazing part of the story—*I got a ministry job offer.*

But this journey wasn't just about a job offer. This was about so much more. After the church service my friend invited me to attend with her, we were discussing my epic saga, and I made a statement I've made many times before: "I know God is trying to teach me something through all this. I just don't know what it is yet."

GOD'S GIFT OF TOUCH
— Lynne Hartke —

BUTTERFLIES NEED THE warming touch of the sun. Their cold-blooded bodies require temperatures of at least 60 degrees (but prefer 82 to 100 degrees) before taking flight. Without the touch of the sun, butterflies will tuck themselves under structures or plants until the temperature rises. Butterflies also bask in sunny spots, their wings spread wide to soak up the sun's rays. Psalm 19:6 (NIV) says of the sun, "It rises at one end of the heavens and makes its circuit to the other; nothing is deprived of its warmth."

Like butterflies, humans can also spread their arms wide in gratitude with the warmth of the sun—and the Son.

She smiled sweetly. "What if God's not simply trying to teach you something? What if He's trying to show His heart for you?"

His heart for me. That was it. That's what He wanted me to see.

His heart for me was provision.

His heart for me was community.

His heart for me was trust.

His heart for me was *good.*

It wasn't control I needed to fix the broken places in my life; it was simply Jesus. And while my hair may still be uncooperative, my grip on my circumstances has loosened with every hard season God walks me through.

It was in this particular season that God also sowed a life verse in my heart: "I know how to live on almost nothing or with everything. I have learned the secret of living in every situation, whether it is with a full stomach or empty, with plenty or little. For I can do everything through Christ, who gives me strength" (Philippians 4:12–13, NLT).

And it is from this season that I birthed the prayer I have prayed continually for myself and now pray over my children, the prayer that I pray over you as well, dear reader: "May you always know that God is good, regardless of your circumstances."

If you consistently experience God's mercy on a daily, ongoing basis, then you know that there are no second chances. There are *infinite* chances.

—T. D. Jakes, pastor

CHAPTER 4

Second Chances

Let Your Dreams
Take Flight

Linda Bartlett

Have you heard of "God winks"? They are times in life when
God acts in a person's life in completely unexpected ways. I feel
my story is full of them and maybe a complete God grin as well.

Becoming a grandmother is one of life's greatest events. I was
thrilled when my eldest son had his first child, my first grand-
baby. I couldn't wait to spoil and love him. There was only one
problem. My son and his family lived in small-town Wisconsin,
and I lived in Atlanta. There would be few opportunities to
babysit and enjoy little Dakota.

My husband worked in government services and made
a decent salary but not enough that we could often fly, on a
whim, to Wisconsin. I was a teacher for a private company in
Marietta, Georgia, that cared for teens who were wards of the
state. It was not the normal public school system with summers,
weekends, and holidays off. These students needed care 24/7,
52 weeks of the year. There were few opportunities for vacation
time.

So along with limited funds, there was also limited time.
I mused about changing things up. Wouldn't it be fun to use
my love of travel to somehow make money? My friends said
I'd be a great tour guide; I loved seeing new places and was

comfortable herding difficult teens around, perfect practice for dealing with adult tourists.

I asked God for answers. Do I leave a job I love for the unknown with hopes that somehow, I could see my grandchild more often? It seemed far-fetched. But, looking back, I can picture a wide grin on God's face as He already had plans in place.

My husband, Jerry, and I had a free getaway weekend to tour time-share condos in Myrtle Beach, South Carolina. I couldn't wait—it was a chance to relax and think. The first thing we did was change into swimsuits and check out the hot tub. We found ourselves sharing it with another couple about the same age. The conversation turned to jobs, and the woman gushed about her new position. She was fifty-three and had just become a flight attendant. How could that be? She was the same age I was and had achieved my long-lost dream.

> Take delight in the LORD, and he will give you the desires of your heart.
>
> —PSALM 37:4 (NIV)

Weren't all flight attendants young, beautiful, and statuesque? Apparently, all the old rules had been thrown out. New laws about age and appearance meant such discrimination was illegal.

"Seriously," I asked, "do they actually hire old grandmas?"

"Yes," she assured me. "Just go and apply."

Thinking about the possibilities was like opening the perfect gift on Christmas morning. I had never dared think this far outside the box. When I was a teen, my dream was to be a "fly girl" with white gloves and an exotic life. The rules at that time required flight attendants to retire at age thirty-two, and you certainly couldn't be married. Plus, you had to be beautiful and poised. All of those qualifications left me out.

I loved teaching and had done it for 30 years, but now the thought of living a childhood dream was as irresistible as a donut to a food junkie.

Once back in Atlanta I picked up the Sunday edition of the *Atlanta Journal*. As I turned to the want ads, an unbelievable sight appeared. There, front and center, was an entire page advertising an airline jobs fair the following weekend in downtown Atlanta.

Coincidence? No, I was sure now God had a hand in this.

I couldn't wait to fly (sorry) down the next Saturday to sign up for my next adventure. All airlines were represented, and people were busy browsing the brochures and filling out applications. As I looked around, I noticed heels and business suits. I'd shown up in sandals and a froufrou dress, the kind of outfit I'd wear for teaching. Big mistake! Now not only did I have age against me but style as well. I had no choice but to put on a huge smile and try to sell myself anyway. Most representatives were not encouraging, but I filled out dozens of applications, hoping God would provide the next miracle.

I went home to wait for that important call, pleading with God that if this was the path (and by the events that had already taken place, I felt it was) that the call would come. Just about the time I wanted to give up, Pinnacle Airlines, a subsidiary of Northwest Airlines, offered me an interview. The interview was in Minneapolis the second week of August.

Believe it or not, I already would be in Minneapolis that week for a wedding. Now I knew, with no doubt, that God had a hand in the events. In the past, it seemed that God took His sweet time in answering prayer, but this time He seemed to move at warp speed. I hadn't really thought this all through. I passed my interview and got the job.

Now, how was I supposed to work in Minneapolis when I lived in Atlanta? My interviewer eased my mind by telling me that I could just take a flight to work and fly back home when I was done. I'd just need a crash pad, someplace to stay overnight between days of work. I had a son who owned a house in the Minneapolis area, and he invited me to stay whenever I needed to. Again, things fell into place.

And then . . .

Class was set to begin on September 11, 2001. Yes, 9/11! No one flew anywhere that day after the towers were hit, of course, and the class was postponed. I decided to trust that God would open the right door at the right time.

Human resources called me and told me they were starting the class in October. Some of those who had originally signed up did not show up. My mother thought I was crazy, but nothing, not even the threat of terrorists, could scare me out of a dream.

> **In him we were also chosen, having been predestined according to the plan of him who works out everything in conformity with the purpose of his will.**
>
> **—EPHESIANS 1:11 (NIV)**

I was sent a long list of city airline codes to memorize along with the safety speeches that flight attendants give on each flight. All had to be memorized before class began. Tough for an old brain already full of teacher jargon.

The class was tough too. No one mentioned serving drinks. It was all about safety equipment, how to use it, and how to run all the safety drills including plane evacuation. Tests were given orally and written. I passed with the help of a considerable amount of study.

> **Jesus looked at them and said, "With man this is impossible, but with God all things are possible."**
>
> —MATTHEW 19:26 (NIV)

As if I had not experienced enough God winks already, I now found out one of the standard flight routes would take me to Appleton, the Wisconsin town where my new grandson lived. I also received the most seniority since I was the oldest in the class, and if you know anything about the airline industry, seniority is everything. It allows you to pick the flight schedule you want. I could work my days in a row and still have half of the month off in Atlanta.

I began the job immediately and stayed for 10 years of fun, living my fantasy. There were trying times like when the Northwest and Delta merger happened, but overall, I had the time of my life.

God has blessed me with the chance to visit all seven continents, all fifty states, and over sixty different countries. Best of all, I had the opportunity to see my grandson every month and watch him grow. I still fly free anywhere in the United States and for a reduced price anywhere outside the US that Delta flies. This perk is mine for the rest of my life.

After 30 years of marriage, three children, numerous teaching jobs, and a grandchild, I had finally achieved a childhood dream, thanks to the "chance" meeting in a hot tub orchestrated by God.

Stirring the Nest

Tez Brooks

I stared through the raindrops on the windowpane. Rats ran up and down the fire escape, ignoring the Central Florida summer downpour in their endless search for food. Inside, my efficiency apartment was dry but lonely. Part of me envied the rodents with their tight-knit family system. I had nobody—or at least it felt that way lately.

My wife had left me again for another man. I felt emasculated, like I'd been thrown into the bargain bin at a dollar store. All I had strived to attain was reduced to a list of assets on the divorce documents.

After 6 years, my career with an insurance company had run its course. I needed a change if I were to break out of this funk. *Lord, point me in the right direction. I need a new job, a better living place, and some gumption.*

A few weeks later, God answered my prayer with a call from my cousin. Wayne was a pastor on Florida's east coast, about 90 minutes from me.

"You interested in working for our church? It's only part-time, but we need a children's ministry director who could double as the janitor."

I hesitated. "I haven't done kids' ministry in 10 years."

"Things haven't changed that much. I think you'd be a good fit. But you'd have to move out here, of course."

We talked about the cost of living, moving expenses, job descriptions, the size of the congregation, and more. I said I would pray about it.

My son and daughter lived with their mom, only 15 minutes away. This made it possible to be with them a lot. I often picked them up from school and had them spend the night at my place a few nights each week. We went to church together every Sunday, and they had barely felt the effects of a broken home. So, the decision to move an hour and a half away was not to be taken lightly.

God often answered my prayers by making choices quite obvious. This time was no exception. Doors started closing for me in Central Florida. My rent went up, and my married friends became distant now that I was single again. It felt like God was kicking me out of town.

Meanwhile, I had the job offer from my cousin in addition to a substitute teacher job in the same city. So when Mark, one of the single guys from Wayne's church, called and asked if I wanted to rent out a room in his house, I started packing.

The move happened quickly. Determined to make this work, my ex-wife and I agreed to start meeting in Orlando, halfway between her place and mine, to exchange the kids each week. Wayne was ready for me to start working at the church right away. My new home with Mark was beautiful, with plenty of bedrooms for my son and daughter when they spent the night. Things were falling into place nicely.

Summer turned into fall, which means nothing in Florida when it comes to weather. The schools started calling me to fill in for absent teachers. But these hours weren't reliable, and being a substitute teacher was hard work. Things on the coast were more expensive than I'd anticipated, and even my role at Wayne's church lacked appeal. Increasingly, my ex found excuses not to be able to make the drive to exchange our kids, so I had to go all the way to her place and back if I wanted my children to spend the weekend.

"Tez, can I take you to lunch today?" Wayne asked one day as I mopped the men's restroom floor.

A few hours later, I was sitting in a Chinese restaurant listening to Wayne break the news that he was resigning from the church to accept a pastorate for a congregation in Orlando.

He continued sharing about his new job, but I had tuned him out. My mind was racing through the few options I had for my own life. I didn't want to stay in that church; the new pastor wouldn't want the former pastor's cousin around. So half my income would be gone if I left, and the teaching gig wasn't reliable enough to float me.

> **You shall live in the region of Goshen and be near me—you, your children and grandchildren, your flocks and herds, and all you have. I will provide for you there.**
>
> —GENESIS 45:10–11 (NIV)

"What do you think, Tez?" Wayne's question snapped me back to the present. "How are you feeling about my family and me moving? You okay with that?"

"Um, I'll figure it out. I'm not your problem. You do what God is calling you to do. I'm excited for you!"

In reality, I was ticked off. While sincere and heartfelt, my cousin's apology didn't change the fact that I had pulled up roots and relocated, thinking this was a long-term decision. I drove home that day, asking God to give me wisdom and peace. But I was a little ticked off at Him too.

So, now what, God? You moved me out here; what's the plan?

The house was empty when I got home. It was Friday, and my roommate had left for the weekend. He had met a woman recently through a Christian dating service and was going to visit her again in Georgia.

I spent Sunday morning listening to Wayne preach and looking around the congregation, trying to imagine myself here without my relatives. There was not one person I had grown close enough to in these few short months to keep me here.

What if I move back to Polk County, God? Plenty of folks there I know and love. It's comfortable.

When I got home, Mark had returned. "Sit down, bro. I gotta tell you something."

"Yeah?"

"I'm engaged!"

"Huh?"

"I asked Sarah to marry me Friday night, and she said yes!"

I tried to match his joy, "Really? Wow, nice."

"Right?"

"You met like, what, couple months ago?"

"Right?" His grin getting wider.

I hadn't known him long enough to tell him he was an idiot. "I'm happy for you."

"Thanks. We're getting married at the courthouse in 3 weeks. She's moving in here after the ceremony."

"Wait, what?"

"How soon can you be out? Maybe Pastor Wayne can let you use his spare room?"

I wasn't about to wait 2 weeks to move out. I wanted to make a statement, so I packed up my stuff that night and went to a hotel.

I'm so "over" this town! This is ridiculous.

The next day I called my old employer, explained my failed attempt to start a new life, and inquired if he might like me back. He was thrilled and asked how soon I could start.

I handed in my resignation to Wayne, advising him I'd be moving the same week he would leave his church. "I'll be closer to my kids again too."

"That's exciting! If you can, you should visit our new church out there."

I wasn't a big fan of Wayne at the moment, but

> **May the Lord direct your hearts into God's love and Christ's perseverance.**
>
> **—2 THESSALONIANS 3:5 (NIV)**

reluctantly, in an attempt to forgive and move on, I agreed to give it a try.

Before long, I found myself gainfully employed and settling into a nice apartment in Orlando. But something worried and embarrassed me. Had I misunderstood God's leading by relocating to the coast? Was this all a massive failure on my part? Maybe it was my fault God had ripped the carpet out from under me.

How will I ever trust myself again to know Your voice, God? Am I even supposed to be here in Orlando now?

One good thing about moving twice was that I was now more flexible regarding change. I visited Wayne's new church and loved the thriving, godly singles' community there. I quickly made friends, jumping into church activities with both feet.

I was not looking for a relationship, nor did I plan to remarry. But at the singles Christmas party only a month later, I met Christine, a young woman in her thirties who had committed her life to being a missionary. She had a similar story of a rough relocation that landed her at this church. We became fast friends.

Way out of my league, Christine was intelligent, gracious, beautiful—and never married!

> **He guarded him as the apple of his eye, like an eagle that stirs up its nest and hovers over its young, that spreads its wings to catch them and carries them aloft.**
>
> **—DEUTERONOMY 32:10–11 (NIV)**

Why hadn't some guy snatched her up by now?

I was drawn to her maturity and dedication to God. My kids loved her too.

Now married to Christine for 22 years with two more daughters together, I look back and marvel that God had a plan all along to prosper my relationships (a beautifully blended family) and my career (serving the Lord in ministry). I would never have met and married this amazing woman had I not obeyed God and relocated. For almost 2 decades, we have been in full-time ministry, living overseas and traveling the world as missionaries. We've watched hundreds come to Christ. My perceived failure was a road to God's purpose and plan for me, and Christine.

I'm reminded of the mother eagle when her babies are ready to fly. She removes the cushioning fluff of her nest, exposing the sticks and making her fledglings uncomfortable, so they venture closer to the edge. They flap their wings with excitement, feeling the lift. Sometimes the mother gives them a little nudge as they prop themselves on the rim. Eventually, the eaglets jump, entering their mother's world among the clouds. They have learned to soar!

It took God stirring up my nest twice to get me to soar. He knew I needed to take it in stages. Did I always trust that God knew what He was doing? No. But that didn't bother God. He kept nudging until I was exactly where He wanted me. This lot in life, first camouflaged as failure, revealed itself as God's perfect plan.

How a Snowstorm Changed My Life

Doug Fannon, as told to Ellen Fannon

My aspiration of becoming an air force pilot depended on meticulous planning, perfect timing, and one critical weekend. And God, of course, but I figured I had everything under control. I prayed He would open the doors for me, and it seemed He had.

From the age of five, I knew I wanted to be a pilot. After high school I enlisted in the army to fly helicopters because flying helicopters as a warrant officer didn't require college. At the time I did not have the desire or the maturity to go to college. But flying jets in the US Air Force became my true objective. Air force fighter pilots must be commissioned officers, which means obtaining a college degree. Although I had taken some college courses while in the army, I was about a year and a half from completing my degree.

In late February of 1980, I realized I had one chance to fly air force jets. Stationed at Fort Campbell, Kentucky, I lived on post, just over the border in Tennessee. At 25 years old, I needed to finish my college degree before I reached twenty-six and a half, the maximum age to start air force flight training.

I had a decision to make. I could stay in the army and fly helicopters as a warrant officer and complete my 20-year military career, or I could complete my obligation to the army, get out in June, and finish my year and a half of college to qualify for the air force. After some investigation, I discovered I could complete my education, earning a bachelor of science degree in aeronautical studies at Embry-Riddle Aeronautical College in Daytona Beach, Florida.

I also inquired about ROTC (Reserved Officer Training Corps). As an army warrant officer, I couldn't get a direct commission into the air force, so I needed to go through officer training. I found I could get my commission at the same time I attended Embry-Riddle.

The opportunity to finish my degree while getting my commission at the same time seemed too good to pass up.

I talked with the ROTC, Embry-Riddle admissions, and the education department at Fort Campbell, and they advised me that if I started school in the summer semester and maxed out my schedule, I could graduate the following May and qualify to fly jets. I had a small window of opportunity and I decided to go for it.

> **Many are the plans in the mind of a man, but it is the purpose of the LORD that will stand.**
>
> **—PROVERBS 19:21 (ESV)**

I finalized my plans and made an appointment for an interview with Embry-Riddle and the ROTC in Daytona Beach for the first weekend in March—my one and only opportunity to get everything lined up and make the application. I organized the whole trip to Florida down to the last detail. I took a few days of leave and, with minimal money, made plans to drive straight through from Northern Tennessee to Daytona Beach, an approximately 12-hour drive.

After flying all day Friday, I came home, packed my bags, and set my alarm to leave before daylight. I planned to get to Daytona Beach by the end of the day and spend the next day looking for a place to live. On Monday I would apply and interview with the college and the ROTC, make all the arrangements to begin school in June as soon as I finished up with the army, and then drive home on Tuesday. I went to bed early.

When I woke up, I discovered a foot of snow had fallen during the night. A snowstorm the first weekend in March in Northern Tennessee was essentially unheard of. A sense of numbing unreality gripped me. I *had* to make this trip or abandon my dream. I set out, determined nothing would stop me from getting to my destination, but the heavy snow made it impossible for me to even make it to the front gate of the army post. Frustrated and discouraged, I turned around and came home, sick that I had lost my one shot. With a heavy heart, I called Daytona Beach and canceled my interviews.

What was God thinking? Why was He working against me? I asked in my heart.

I threw more than just a little resentment God's way. After all, He was the One who put the passion to fly in my heart. Why had my plans lined up so perfectly if He was just going to slam the door to my dream in my face? Why, of all weekends, when He knew how important it was for me to make this trip, did He send this snowstorm? Especially in a place and season when snow was almost unprecedented.

On Monday morning, filled with defeat, I trudged to the education center on post, into the office of the Embry-Riddle adviser, and explained what had happened. I doubted if anything I had worked for could be salvaged at this point. Nevertheless, although I felt as if I'd landed back at square one, I hoped they would be able to help in some way. The adviser suggested we take a look at what might be available on-post.

It turned out that the education center at Fort Campbell conformed to the army's 7-week training cycles. Soldiers spent 7 weeks in the field, then 7 weeks in garrison, during which time they could attend classes, thus completing their education. Semesters consisted of 7-week accelerated cycles. When we looked at the available courses, we found I could complete all courses required by Embry-Riddle for a bachelor of science degree in aeronautical studies by December—a full 6 months earlier than I would in Daytona Beach!

> **You also must be ready, because the Son of Man will come at an hour when you do not expect him.**
>
> **—LUKE 12:40 (NIV)**

I joined the Tennessee Army National Guard, which needed helicopter pilots to fill open slots. Being in the national guard enabled me to receive special permission to continue my schooling at the on-post education center, even though I was no longer on active duty in the army. Not only did my school schedule work out better than if I had gone to Daytona Beach, but I also had a job and I didn't even have to move.

Who would have thought that a snowstorm derailing my carefully laid plans would have turned out to be a good thing?

After getting out of the army in June and joining the national guard, I went to school on the Fort Campbell post during the week and flew for the Guard on the weekends. In the fall, prior to graduating in December, I applied for Officer's Training School (OTS) with the air force and got approved and accepted for air force flight training. In January I started OTS at Lackland Air Force Base (AFB) in San Antonio, Texas, and obtained my commission as a second lieutenant in April. One week later, I started air force flight training at Laughlin AFB, in Del Rio, Texas.

Over the next 18 years, I went on to fly numerous fighters, including A-7s, AT-38s, and F-16s. I have been blessed to have one of the most unique careers in the military, starting as a helicopter pilot with the army and finishing as a T-34 instructor pilot, flying with the navy in primary flight training.

Ask and it will be given to you; seek and you will find; knock and the door will be opened to you.

—MATTHEW 7:7 (NIV)

After retiring from 25 years in the military, God led me into full-time Christian ministry. In 2010 I graduated from the New Orleans Baptist Theological Seminary with my master of divinity degree. I now serve as the senior pastor in a small church in Florida.

There is no doubt in my mind that God sent that freak snowstorm to thwart my plans because He had something better for me. As I look back on that event, I am filled with a sense of wonder that the Creator of the universe cared so much about the details of my life that He used such a drastic measure to direct me down a different path.

GOD'S GIFT OF SIGHT
— Heidi Gaul —

A CAREFREE DAISY blowing in the wind. A cat's effortless grace. Drops of morning dew on the grass. If you're like me, you see God in these and other everyday moments. Most gracious and rare are those times He offers us a private glimpse of the majesty of His creation. The transcendent splendor of a flock of geese soaring overhead. The passion of waves crashing in their endless caress of the shore. Sights like these feel personal, gifts too personal to share. There are no words to describe that divine communion—only wonder and gratitude for what we can see with our eyes and feel with our heart.

At the time, in my disappointment and frustration, I couldn't see that God had better plans for me than the ones I had so painstakingly prepared. But He showed me His ways are always the best.

Did God Want Me to Be Homeless?

Marilyn Turk

"We're going to have to let you go. We'll accompany you to your desk so you can retrieve whatever belongs only to you."

I stared at the man delivering this message, my heart thumping, as the reality of that cold statement reverberated throughout my body.

Twenty-five years—half my life—had been devoted to this company. But ever since my former company was bought out by another, larger company, the climate had changed. Many of my former associates were no longer there. Most had jumped ship when the merger was announced or had been let go afterward, but I had stayed put, believing I was safe. Now I worked for strangers.

With the merger, the company had too many employees, so too often on Fridays, people were let go, calling it a "reduction in force." We called it Black Friday. I hated to see so many good employees lose their jobs, yet I had been certain my seniority would save me.

But this time, it was my turn to get cut.

The new management had no idea what I'd done to grow the business, the awards I'd won, the experience I had, or the knowledge I possessed. They didn't care. I was just a number, one employee too many.

Shock held back my tears as I packed to leave. The associate who watched me as I gathered my belongings seemed uncomfortable with the assignment. He whispered about the unfairness of the decision and joked about the ridiculous likelihood that I would want to steal such things as a company stapler. But I couldn't laugh. I felt like I had been betrayed by the company and was being treated like a criminal.

As I drove away, I prayed about what to do next. I needed to work to support my family— my three sons in college and my home. Since I had gone through a divorce the previous year, the whole burden weighed on my shoulders.

My mind raced, trying to think of whom to contact for help finding another job. Since I knew many people in the business, and with my successful track record, I had no doubt I'd find another job. Thankfully, I would receive 6-month severance pay, which should give me plenty of time to land another one.

> **"For I know the plans I have for you," declares the LORD, "plans to prosper you and not to harm you, plans to give you hope and a future."**
>
> **—JEREMIAH 29:11 (NIV)**

I began calling former associates and people I knew at other companies, but there were few leads on other jobs. I searched employment opportunities with national companies, including those requiring overnight travel because my children were no longer at home. I even applied with another branch of my previous company, but the job would require relocating to a city I did not like, so I wasn't interested.

Surely in a city as large as Atlanta, where I lived, I could find another position. But the only positions I saw offered much lower salaries than I had earned before, salaries too small to pay my bills. I was told that business was suffering the effects of a recession. So was I.

The only benefit of having so much free time was that I could attend weekly Bible studies I hadn't been able to attend when I was working. I always try to look for God's purpose in things that happen, so I joined one, then two, then three, trying to fill my time with spiritual growth. In the Bible, I read Scripture about waiting on God and not worrying about anything, trusting God to take care of me. So I tried to focus on that assurance.

But as days without work passed into months, anxiety moved in, robbing me of the trust I had in God. Every morning I met with Him at my kitchen table and prayed, asking for direction. What had I done wrong? What was I supposed to do now? But it seemed like God wasn't listening. I wondered if I'd been "put out to pasture" as they do with old horses who could no longer work. Was that it? Was I now past my usefulness?

During that time, two promising job positions opened up, and my hope returned. I applied, flying out of state for one of the interviews. I left each interview feeling I would be hired but then found out a few days later that I'd been the second choice behind two younger, less-experienced people.

When my best friend suggested I sell my home and downsize, I couldn't imagine that as an answer. "After all, you don't need a large house anymore with your kids in school." Maybe not, but I'd never intended to move from that home. Through some miraculous events 10 years before, I knew God had given me this house I'd prayed for. Why would He want me to move out of it now? And since it was the home of my dreams, I had no desire to live elsewhere and had long envisioned my future grandchildren coming there to visit. Besides, where would I go?

But when my severance pay ran out, I was forced to dip into my savings, wondering how much longer I could keep paying for my house with no job on the horizon. The future looked grim as I realized I might lose my house anyway. Did God want me to be homeless?

> **If you remain in me and my words remain in you, ask whatever you wish, and it will be done for you.**
>
> **—JOHN 15:7 (NIV)**

Finally, a business friend of mine offered me a job that paid less than I needed, because he believed that potential employers would prefer to hire someone who was working and not one who was unemployed. I took the position as I continued to look for another one. That position put me in contact with other businesses out of state, and someone at a meeting I attended offered to take my résumé back to his state.

The handwriting was on the wall. I would have to do something different and consider relocating, which meant selling my beloved home. I finally offered it back to God, trusting Him to provide another one for me.

When I relinquished the one thing I wanted to hold on to, the doors began to open, and I was offered three jobs in

Alabama. I accepted one, put my house on the market, and began looking for another home in another state.

Timing had to be perfect, or I would be stuck with two house payments. But I had to totally trust God to work things out. It became clear to me that He wanted me to move, so here I was, working a new position in one state while selling my house in another and commuting back and forth. Once my training was complete, I'd be working in Florida for the new company, so I had to find a home there.

Two months later, I put in an offer on a condo in Florida before my home in Atlanta sold. When the condo closed a month later, I found myself traveling between three states— Georgia, Alabama, and Florida—but I still didn't have two mortgage payments due at once.

Naysayers shook their heads at my situation, but I told them God would work it out. He was the one who started it, and He would finish it. I had peace that He would, so I wouldn't consider any other options.

When my Atlanta Realtor told me there was an offer on my house, I accepted it, but I couldn't leave work for the closing in Georgia. However, he worked things out so that I participated in the meeting on the phone while driving between Birmingham and Florida. In God's perfect timing, I ended up with only one house payment.

But why did God relocate me? Why did He want me to move? I was now single, living alone for the first time in 23 years. I knew no one in Florida, but I wanted to be part of a local church. Church was where I would fit in with others, even if I didn't know anyone. The first church I attended in my new hometown was friendly and welcoming, giving me no reason to look anywhere else.

As a single woman, though, I couldn't find a Sunday class to attend. All the small groups were for married couples. Even when I had been married in Atlanta, I attended a women's class at my church. But this church didn't offer a class just for women, so I suggested they add one. A few weeks later, I received a phone call from the church's minister of education about my suggestion. Surprisingly, she asked me if I'd like to lead such a class. I was shocked because I was a newcomer. But I believed there was a need, and since I had taught a women's class in my former church, I accepted.

> **And we know that in all things God works for the good of those who love him, who have been called according to his purpose.**
>
> —ROMANS 8:28 (NIV)

The Sunday of our first meeting, a man came to the door of the room, introduced himself, and welcomed me. His name was Chuck Turk, and as I looked into his eyes, I saw that he was a good man. Over the next few months, he continued to drop by and say hello. I learned from others that he was a widower and dating the pianist at church. Something inside me cried out to God that I wanted to marry a man like that someday.

Several months later, he asked me out on a date. Turns out the other lady had been only a friend. Soon Chuck and I were in love, 8 months later we were married, and I finally understood why God had relocated me. He had a new life waiting for me, a new home, and a new purpose. All I had to do was trust Him.

GOD'S GIFT OF TASTE
— Buck Storm —

MY MOM ALWAYS baked an angel food cake on my birthday—my favorite. When I think of comfort food, this one tops my list. To this day, the taste of angel food is the taste of home.

I believe God loves to give us tastes of our future home as well. A perfect sunset, distant mountains, light slanting across a desert valley, great music—these are things that never fail to transport me in my heart to what will be my final address.

Angel food in heaven? Who knows, but I think so. Maybe we'll eat it together.

A Clean Bill of Slate

Kristy Dewberry

My new husband and I were on the verge of bankruptcy. We'd gotten ourselves into a pickle, or, more accurately, I'd gotten us both into a pickle. Not from student loans, online gambling, or credit card debt, but because I'd decided to open an art store. It had seemed like a no-brainer a year earlier, but now it seemed like a half-brainer.

I had met my husband, Don, while working for his mom and stepdad at one of their arts-and-crafts stores in Oklahoma City. It was the perfect job for an art major. I received a discount on the never-ending list of required school supplies, and I had a flexible schedule to work around my classes.

I'd been working at their shop since I was 18 years old but didn't meet Don until I was twenty-one, when he moved to Oklahoma City to work as an accountant for his parents. I happened to run into him at their warehouse where I was picking up supplies to restock the shelves. I passed by his small office and smiled at him. He claims it was a flirtatious grin. Probably so. I knew by the way his eyes lit up that he was interested. I told a coworker that he would be calling me to ask me out on a date soon. It took him less than an hour.

Don was a few years older than I was. I'd had my heart broken several times in the past because I had a knack for choosing the wrong kind of man. Suddenly I was dating the right kind of man. He had a real job, unlike some of the men I'd dated. He made me feel safe, special, and cared for.

I remember the very second I fell in love with him. I was at his apartment and the phone book was open on the kitchen table. He had doodled a heart on the page with "I love Kris" on it. I tore out the page and have kept it locked in my keepsake drawer for 40 years.

After a year of marriage, I decided I'd like to open my own art store. His stepdad could be difficult to work for and I was ready for a change. It wasn't as though we had no other income. If we had a slow month we could rely on Don's salary to pay the bills. How hard could it be?

Famous last words.

I didn't do my research. I chose a spot at an overpriced strip mall in a high-income location in Edmond, Oklahoma. The rent was outrageously high, compared to Oklahoma City, but I was sure that the art students from the local college would swarm in to buy their supplies. We ordered a large lighted sign that set us back another gazillion bucks and had our (not-so) grand opening. A few people trickled in to see what was up, then trickled back out again.

One of the "tricklers" was the zone-enforcement guy who informed us that our sign didn't meet their code. He gave us two choices. We could remove the sign or we could rehang it facing the brick wall of the shop next to ours, making it impossible to see. It was a ridiculous ordinance, and we fought the law, but the law won. We had to rely on word-of-mouth from customers who just happened to find us while walking by the other stores. Also, no art students came by. Another art store had already made a deal with the university.

We struggled through the first year. Our meager profits went toward the lease and utilities. Fortunately, my husband still had his accounting job. He'd work eight to five, then race to the store to frame pictures, which turned out to be the only profitable part of the business. We would sometimes be up until two in the morning, drive 30 minutes home, then repeat the next day. Even with that, we were falling behind on the business bills.

Then, with little advance notice, my in-laws closed their business. Suddenly Don was out of work, so our only source of income was gone. We didn't panic. He'd just find another accounting job. No problem, or so we assumed. He immediately updated his résumé and applied for every accounting job in the *Daily Oklahoman*'s want ads.

> **But seek first the kingdom of God and His righteousness, and all these things shall be added to you.**
>
> **—MATTHEW 6:33 (NKJV)**

After receiving zero responses, we panicked just a bit, so he branched out to include lower-paying jobs, like accounts payable. Nothing. He began applying for anything and everything. A minimum wage job would be better than nothing. Cell phones didn't yet exist, so we relied on the answering machine at home.

If the message light was blinking when we got home from the store, we'd get our hopes up that it was a response with a job offer or a request to schedule an interview. But the only messages were from utility companies threatening to cut off services and our mortgage company warning us that our house payments were overdue. I applied for jobs as well. Whoever got a job first, the other would keep the store open, at least temporarily.

He mentioned bankruptcy, but I didn't want to go that route if we could help it. I stubbornly refused to give up on my dream. I was raised in a family that handled our problems without help from others. However, we were two months late on our lease and would be evicted soon if something didn't happen quickly.

I made an appointment with a loan officer at the bank across the street from the store. Maybe I could get a loan to help catch up on our lease payments. As I sat in front of the imposing man and his oversized desk, I tried to be very adult until the moment that I stammered that I needed a loan to "turn over a clean bill of slate." The banker was so amused at my jumbled metaphors of a clean slate, a clean bill of health, and turning over a new leaf, that he approved the loan.

The bank loan turned out to be just a piece of duct tape on a flat tire. It slowed the leak temporarily but then we were right back where we started.

I wasn't raised in a Christian home, even though I'd always believed in God in my own lazy way. Don had been raised in a strict Christian family, but he hadn't attended church since we met. He'd shared his beliefs and mentioned a few times that he missed going to church, but I kept putting him off.

He finally asserted himself. "We need God, and we need a church family. We can't do this on our own. It's not working. Let's pray that God shows us the right church for us." He took my hands in his and prayed that God would help us out of this financial situation and that He would give us the right church home.

As he prayed, the word *Trinity* came into my mind and I got goose bumps (or maybe God bumps?) Did I just hear from God? When I told Don, he got out the yellow pages and looked up churches named Trinity. Turns out there were a whole lot of churches with Trinity in the name. I was disappointed. Maybe I didn't hear from God after all.

A few days later, a woman came to the store to purchase some craft supplies. She exuded joy, and I found myself laughing with her. Before she left, she invited us to attend her church. Trinity Church. We did and I felt God's presence as soon as we entered.

As we sang with the rest of the congregation, my eyes filled with tears. The sermon about trusting in God resonated with me. Trusting in myself wasn't working so well. Maybe it was time to admit that I couldn't handle everything by myself. I needed help. Maybe God was the one to provide it.

> Set your minds on things above, not on earthly things.
>
> —COLOSSIANS 3:2 (NIV)

❧

"God," I prayed. "You know how stubborn I am and how hard it is for me to admit I need help. But we need help. I don't know why Don isn't not getting any response to his résumés. Please find him the perfect job and help me out of the financial bind I got us into with this store."

A few days later, our store phone rang, and when the man at the other end asked for Don, I assumed it was a question about picture framing. I passed the phone to Don and his puzzled expression changed to one of astonishment. As soon as he hung up, he hugged me.

"That was an office supply business. They want me to come in for an interview tomorrow."

"But how did they get our store number?" I asked.

"I have no idea. In fact, I didn't even apply there. The whole thing is crazy."

Don was hired on the spot. The man who called was the prior office accounting manager and was hiring his own replacement. It turned out to be the perfect job for Don. He earned a good income and we finally had health insurance and benefits. None of the jobs we'd hoped for would have been the right one. God knew exactly what we needed and He provided it. He just was waiting for us to ask.

> "Consider carefully what you hear," he continued. "With the measure you use, it will be measured to you—and even more."
>
> —MARK 4:24 (NIV)

Soon after Don took over the office, he found a stack of résumés of all the people who had applied for his job. They were stuck in a manila folder in the bottom drawer of the desk. Of course, Don's résumé wasn't in there. He had never applied for this position. There is no explanation other than God answering our prayers.

We did close down our art store eventually, and were able to avoid bankruptcy and make sure all our debtors were paid in full. I'm still an entrepreneur. Decades later, I have an eBay store and I am a freelance writer, but now I trust in God, not

GOD'S GIFT OF SMELL
— Lynne Hartke —

AFTER A RAINSTORM, southwestern deserts have a distinct aroma. When people say, "I love the smell of the desert after the rain," they are not just talking about the clean atmosphere. Yes, the dust has been washed away from every surface—from the prickliest cactus to the tiniest wildflower. But rain also releases a pungent aroma from the creosote bush, a tough desert survivor. The resinous armor on the leaves shields the plant from heat, but once moistened, a marvelous scent perfumes the air. The creosote bush is a fragrant reminder of God's promise to send rain to desert places.

myself. We no longer try to do everything on our own or wait until we've exhausted every resource before we turn to God. We turn to God first. With His help, we were able to "turn over a clean bill of slate."

Where We Needed to Go

Sara Etgen-Baker

Brrriiiing! Brrriiiing! Brrriiiing! The telephone yanked me from
my sleep. "Hello," I answered in a groggy voice. "Oh, hi, Bub.
What's going on?" Bub was my brother-in-law, a good friend,
and a teacher in another Texas town across the state.

"Sorry to call and wake you so early, but I have a time-
sensitive opportunity for you. Yesterday, one of the English
teachers in my school district resigned, leaving the district
in quite a bind. Didn't you always want to teach high school
English? I think you're the perfect match! Are you game?"

"Oh my, Bub. That's a tempting proposition." I said reluctantly. "Let me mull it over."

"Okay, but one more thing. School starts in less than 2 weeks.
English teachers are hard to find in our neck of the woods, and
we need to fill this position ASAP."

"All right. I understand. I'll talk it over with Bill and call
you back tomorrow."

I had been at a crossroads in life—complacent and dissatis-
fied, yearning to find my true purpose in life, and praying for
work that impassioned me. Now I faced another immediate
crossroads that demanded a quick, life-changing decision. If
I said yes, I would have to leave behind everything that was
familiar and comfortable and move a thousand miles across
the state.

"Is this a door opening?" I asked my husband. "Is this opportunity an answer to my yearnings, my prayers?" We held each other's hands, closed our eyes, and surrendered ourselves to God and seeking His guidance. And we felt the answer was yes.

A few short days later, we had packed up the life we had enjoyed in this location. Today was moving day, an exciting new beginning. The day everything would change.

"You coming, babe?" Bill asked after loading the last of the boxes into the moving truck. I took one last look at the house, then closed the door with a sharp thud. I quickly clambered into the truck before I changed my mind. One mile forward, then another, and another. The road before us was full of hope, taking us to our new life even as it left our old one behind.

> For everyone who asks receives; the one who seeks finds; and to the one who knocks, the door will be opened.
>
> —MATTHEW 7:8 (NIV)

Within a few days, I found myself inside my first high school classroom feeling both skittish and terrified. My classroom was barren save for a small metal desk and a bookcase, decrepit with age and peeling Formica. Dog-eared hardbacks, many missing covers, scattered in ramshackle order across one of its shelves, their dust jackets missing. Tattered paperbacks, their corners curled, teetered haphazardly on top of one another like a game of Jenga. Oddly, none of them were in English.

"Are you there?" Someone banged on my door. It was Penny, the English department chair. "I have your literature books!" She pushed a cart toward me, parking it adjacent to my desk. "Remember: your freshmen must look at these every day; they must write in their journals twice a week and"—Penny squared her shoulders—"one more thing. The curriculum guide is in your desk. I expect you to follow it. *No exceptions!* It'll take your students where they need to go. Understand?"

"Yes, ma'am," I replied robotically, not wanting to get off on the wrong foot with my new boss.

I placed a literature book on top of each scarred desk, then slid into one of them. I opened the monstrous volume, its contents captivating me—classic short stories, ancient myths, *Romeo and Juliet*, and excerpts from *The Odyssey*. The morning bell sounded, jangling my nerves and jarring me from my seat. Within minutes, rambunctious freshmen hurried past me and took their seats. The tardy bell rang; they settled down; the school year officially began.

During that first week, I followed the curriculum guide as instructed. Monday, I lectured on the five elements of fiction, my students copying my notes from the chalkboard into their notebooks. Tuesday, I read aloud from the literature book, my students turning a page whenever I did. When I asked questions, some students raised their hands and answered; most, though, just nodded and smiled. During Wednesday's journal-writing activity, some students wrote; most just smiled, pretending to write. Although fidgety, my students were quiet, respectful, and compliant. Their faces were full of eagerness, the kind of eagerness a teacher longs for.

On Thursday, even after the air conditioner in my classroom stalled, I continued reading aloud from the literature book. The August sun perched over the Chihuahan Desert, pouring its hot oranges and reds into the sky, making my classroom beastly hot.

My freshmen squirmed in their seats, so I ushered them outside to a nearby bench where they nestled around me like eager baby ducklings. I resumed reading. But then one of my students stood up, pointed to the west, and shouted, "*El Diablo, la profesora! El Diablo!*"

I shaded my eyes and peered across the desert. A trio of dust devils materialized in the distance—looking like columns of whirling smoke, gnawing across the *despoblado*, the barren no-man's-land between the high school and nearby Mexico.

> **Show me your ways, LORD, teach me your paths.**
>
> —PSALM 25:4 (NIV)

"El Diablo!" Another student tugged on my shirt sleeve, "*Trae mala suerte!*"

"What?" I frantically shook my head. "I don't understand!"

"El Diablo trae mala suerte!" *The devil brings bad luck!*

But I didn't know then what they were saying. I politely nodded and smiled, mimicking my students' behavior. At that moment, I realized that I'd mistaken their smiles, nods, and silent compliance as comprehension. The now obvious truth was, I was teaching in a border community where most of my students spoke no English; I spoke no Spanish. My students' eagerness tugged on my heartstrings, though. I desperately wanted to teach them English. I was at yet another crossroads, not knowing how to teach them.

"God," I prayed, "I can't do this on my own. I seek Your help. What is it You'd have me to do? What is Your will?"

Later that afternoon while standing in line at the grocery store, I riffled through the magazine rack and stumbled upon a comic book. I thumbed through it, attracted to its colorful pages, action scenes, and easy-to-read dialogue. I was about to return it to the rack when it occurred to me that it contained many literary fundamentals, archetypes, and the hero's journey.

Aha! God heard my prayer and gave me a solution to my predicament! But what about the literature book and curriculum? Abandoning them wouldn't bode well with Penny and was certainly a risk. I was excited, though, emboldened with purpose and the possibility of being able to reach my students and teach them English.

I purchased every comic book I could find and took them to my classroom. I borrowed concepts from the existing curriculum and created my own using comic books as the context for teaching simple vocabulary, simple grammar, sentence structure, dialogue, myths, the hero archetype, and the elements of fiction. By semester's end, my students were confidently reading and constructing sentences in English.

Despite their progress, my freshmen still couldn't read from the ninth-grade literature book—a fact that displeased Penny. "I told you to use the textbook and curriculum guide. No exceptions. Instead, you undermined me with your unconventional tactics. Why? What were you thinking?"

"I remember your telling me that the textbook and curriculum would take my students where they needed to go. I believed you and wanted to do as you asked, but my students spoke and read no English. Without their speaking English, I couldn't take them where they needed to go until I got them to where they were supposed to be. But you're right." I tried to appease her. "I was wrong in not bringing my plan to you. Please understand, I was desperate to teach them English. I was not ill-intentioned."

"Ill-intentioned or not, I'm not recommending you be rehired." She stormed out of my room.

Figuring I had nothing to lose, I packed away the ninth-grade literature books, replacing them with some seventh-grade readers I'd unearthed in the bookroom. By year's end, my students easily read at the seventh-grade level. They were increasingly confident and performed better in their other classes too. How far they'd come! Even so, at my end-of-the year review, I expected harsh words from my principal followed by a non-renewed contract.

"I don't agree with your unorthodox methodology," she began, "but I admire your willingness to take risks on your students' behalf. I'm pleased with their progress. So I'm renewing your contract—with one condition: You agree to teach English to the same students until they graduate."

I agreed. With God's guidance and help, I took my students from where they were to where they needed to be. After their graduation, I reflected upon the circumstances that brought us together and the 4 years we shared.

> **For if the willingness is there, the gift is acceptable according to what one has, not according to what one does not have.**
>
> **—2 CORINTHIANS 8:12 (NIV)**

How often God's blessings come disguised—as an unexpected answer, an unwelcomed opportunity, or a challenge that requires us to seek His strength and help. In retrospect, I saw how God's loving hand guided and directed me in such a way that took me—and my students—from where we were to where we needed to be.

To sow a tiny black watermelon seed and see a harvest of hundreds of watermelons is to witness the miraculous. Every day we are surrounded by God's abundance and his magnificence; miracles aren't things we *create* but what we *discover* and *experience*.

—Joshua Choonmin Kang, pastor and author

CHAPTER 5

Signs and Wonders

Thank God for Unanswered Prayer

Steve Watkins

There is a certain stillness in the air that precedes bad weather in Tornado Alley. When you grow up on a farm, as I did, watching the weather is something that's just sort of bred into you—a trait that never goes away.

The early morning of Friday, December 10, 2021, exemplified those conditions that farmers know so well. The winds weren't just calm. They were nonexistent, and leaves clung to trees without movement like a deer protecting its young. The sounds of the local landscape on that humid morning were beyond silent. Forecasters had predicted turbulent weather for days. And there were no storms on the horizon yet, but they were coming. The conditions were too perfect. The state weather bureau placed northern Arkansas under a tornado watch (meaning conditions are favorable for severe thunderstorms and tornadoes) by nine a.m.

I spent most of that day at the local weekly newspaper office where I covered politics and human interest and penned a weekly column. Friday traditionally kept me writing all day in preparation for "production Monday" when we laid out the paper for printing that evening for a Tuesday distribution. It had been a long work week and I was eager to finish out the day, get home, and secure our property for whatever we'd face through the night. By noon, the most up-to-date forecast indicated a long pattern of storms forming around five p.m. and likely lasting through the night.

The common knowledge of impending bad weather made it a surprise when local Justice of the Peace Stan Landers called me shortly after noon. Stan planned to host a small party that evening and invited me to join the guests. All good reason said to politely decline Stan's offer and get home as quickly as possible that day. But the journalist in me also knew Stan's position as one of the most influential people in Stone County. Rejecting the invitation might be awkward, and Stan was a nice guy anyway. As my head and my heart said no, my mouth somehow said, "See you at six." I left work and went home to the place my wife and I call "Tranquility Base."

> **Now to Him who is able to do immeasurably more than all we ask or imagine, according to his power that is at work within us.**
>
> **—EPHESIANS 3:20 (NIV)**

Eighteen months earlier I'd been on a mission to secure a small piece of lakefront property in Tiptonville, Tennessee, on Reelfoot Lake. I longed for a second home there where I could get away, fish, and write, and I believed I'd found the perfect spot among Reelfoot's cypress-dotted shoreline.

Four months later, the property owner and I found ourselves at an impasse over the price of the small parcel, no closer than we'd been from the beginning. I offered every creative deal I could imagine. He was only interested in a number.

A few days later in my morning quiet time, something happened. After days of wrestling with ideas and possible offers that would close the deal on my dream, I felt an abrupt and unexpected peace in my spirit. I sensed God encouraging me to move on and stop wasting time. It was as if I could hear His voice.

Move on.

A divine plan unfolded just 2 weeks later as a Realtor drove us through the Ozark region of Arkansas to several acres of riverfront property the locals call Round Bottom Valley. It is an impressive expanse of several dozen acres bordered by the White River to the north and its amazing limestone bluffs to the east. Mountains finish out the horizon to the south and west. Geographically, it's like a big bowl of heaven.

> **In God, whose word I praise—in God I trust and am not afraid. What can mere mortals do to me?**
>
> **—PSALM 56:4 (NIV)**

When I stepped out of the Realtor's pickup truck that November Sunday afternoon, I knew we were home. We bought the property and started construction immediately on a lodge and riverside pavilion, giving birth to our 20-acre homestead.

That Friday afternoon I left work and went home to Tranquility Base. I had just enough time to grab a shower, iron some clothes, and get to Stan's on time. By five p.m., the air in Round Bottom Valley was as thick as soup. You could see signs of storms moving in from the west. I decided I'd arrive at Stan's, shake a few hands, and slip out unnoticed after an hour to get back home where I belonged. It seemed like a reasonable plan.

By six, lightning illuminated the sky constantly. It seemed especially eerie from the elevation of the wraparound porch on Stan's mansion, which was perched atop one of the county's highest elevations. The porch offered a 360-degree view of the developing storm across three counties.

But it was the image on the big-screen television that caught my eye and first gave me real concern. A huge line of powerful storms moved across northeast Arkansas near Monette where I grew up. The screen showed every color on the radar spectrum.

Forecasters had predicted the scenario perfectly. The radar image across all of Arkansas appeared ominous. That next morning at Tranquility Base, we'd barely received a few small stones of hail and some rain. But a powerful tornado that tracked through Monette and northeasterly across six states made national news.

> You will hear a word spoken behind you, saying, "This is the correct way, walk in it," whether you are heading to the right or the left.
>
> —ISAIAH 30:21 (NET)

In the dark hours after it passed through Monette, the storm system tracked northeasterly for another 200 miles, its most ominous display of power and unpredictability in Tiptonville, Tennessee, a community with a major state park and dozens of camping grounds populated by hundreds of RVs, motor homes, and campers.

The scenes in Tiptonville and around Reelfoot Lake that morning are difficult to capture in words. It was as if a giant

GOD'S GIFT OF HEARING
— Heidi Gaul —

HEARING. MANY DIFFERENT sounds come to mind when we think of that word. Some sources say that our ears can pick up fifteen hundred separate tones. This number stretches far beyond my imagination and enters the realm of miraculous.

Like a master conductor, God has orchestrated a world of sound, from a baby's cry to a whisper in the wind to the words, "It is finished," declared from a cross. He speaks to us through laughter and rushing waves, roaring thunder and the buzz of a bee. We have ears for a reason. Let's listen to all He has created.

hand swept through the camping parks and crumpled the motorhomes into big, compressed balls. The ground was swept clean but for a few utility lines dangling out of the hundreds of concrete pads.

With both concern and curiosity, I traveled to Tiptonville about a week later, where what I'd feared was confirmed. The property that I'd wanted so desperately had been destroyed in the tornado, transforming the area into an unrecognizable environment. As we drove toward it, my heart sank.

We might have been there.

When we stopped, I closed my eyes and thanked God for His direction months earlier. I'd wanted the Tiptonville lakefront lot so badly, but God, in all His wisdom, had orchestrated not only a peaceful resolution to a challenging situation but also a peace-filled home we call Tranquility Base.

Embracing the Unexplainable

Nancy Hoag

I used to declare that there was no way we could sense the presence of a loved one who had died. I also believed we couldn't simply "know" a thing that we couldn't see, taste, smell, touch, or hear.

But that was before two experiences that changed forever how I look at death—and God's presence in my life.

Betty was the one friend who had always been there for me. After going through a crippling divorce, I had stopped believing in a loving God. Then, by chance, I met Betty.

She would come to my house, dial my radio to a Christian station, and tell me (like a mother to her child), "Do *not* turn this off!" She read Scripture to me from her well-worn Bible, introduced to me other Spirit-filled women, and encouraged me to pursue and develop my music.

For years, I had been hearing melodies in my spirit, although I couldn't exactly call myself a songwriter or composer. With Betty's support and backing, I began writing down the music and lyrics that had been popping into my head. The words and melodies spoke to me, soothing and comforting me. My confidence grew.

Betty would arrive at my front door several times each week, pour herself a cup of tea, and sit quietly on my sofa while

I played each new tune and told her how my music was changing my mind about God.

Betty not only inspired me to play my new music, but she also visibly reminded me of God's love.

When she died, I was devastated. I felt alone all over again . . . until one rainy morning after I had poured myself a cup of tea and started playing the piano. Suddenly, I became aware of Betty's presence. No, I didn't see her and I didn't even have the nerve to turn around to see if she was in "her place" on the sofa. But I knew and whispered, "I miss you."

When I had finished playing, I realized I was again alone. But there was not an ounce of doubt in me: Betty had been there, and I had been blessed to feel again her acceptance, her encouragement, and even her joy.

A few years later, I was writing at my desk and watching three horses graze on the other side of our road. All of a sudden, I heard myself sing out, "Hi, Grandpa!" I froze. I couldn't type. I couldn't turn around. But I knew my grandpa, one of only a handful of people who had made me feel wholly loved as a child, was grinning as he entered my cozy home office.

> **But in your hearts revere Christ as Lord. Always be prepared to give an answer to everyone who asks you to give the reason for the hope that you have. But do this with gentleness and respect,**
>
> **—1 PETER 3:15 (NIV)**

As a sweet peace hugged me, I recalled how my grandfather had made me feel safe and even happy in my otherwise turbulent and frightening childhood. He was my first music teacher, showing me how to pound out chords on an upright piano while he accompanied me with his fiddle or guitar. I remembered it was important to him that I felt good about my music.

> **For we live by faith, not by sight.**
>
> —2 CORINTHIANS 5:7 (NIV)

As I recalled those times with my grandfather, I knew God wanted me to realize I wasn't alone. I hadn't seen Grandpa with my own eyes, nor had I heard his voice, but he was there. For only seconds, for only so long as I had the breath to say "Hi!"—and then he was gone.

Today, do I fully understand why or how such things happen? I do not. But I can't deny the fact that I did "know" Betty and Grandpa had visited with me. I knew even without turning around to "see" them.

Life has thrown me other curveballs, times when I've felt upended, out of balance, lost in life. But then—and now—I know I'm never truly alone. God fills me with a sense of His own presence, along with the knowledge that not only am I not alone, but I am—and forever will be—loved.

Small Beginnings

Kristen West

All I wanted was to make a difference in the world. But life kept getting in the way.

I was 17 years old when I gave my life to Christ. I knew very quickly that I wanted my life to impact the world for Him. Vocational ministry seemed like the obvious choice. I didn't know all it entailed, but, to me, working in a church would be the pinnacle of public service for God.

Then I got pregnant. I had married shortly after graduating from high school, and my first daughter was born a little more than a year later. I was delighted and poured myself into being the best mother I could be. Three years later, we welcomed a son.

I was a stay-at-home mom, completely consumed with diapers, toys, piles of laundry, and visits to the local park. I poured myself into Bible studies and growing in my personal walk with God. Deep down, though, I longed to do something "bigger."

Several years went by. My first marriage failed, and my children and I entered a decade-long period of just trying to survive. I took as many part-time jobs as I could and worked tirelessly to keep food on the table, gas in the car, and God in my heart.

Following this season of singleness, I remarried. My new husband had been a single father of two little children himself. Our union was reminiscent of *The Brady Bunch* and the six of us embarked on trying to figure out exactly what "family" meant now.

We struggled through myriad blended family issues, including favoritism, and more hurts and misunderstandings than I can begin to count. I wrestled with being grateful for where God had brought me while internally questioning His wisdom in fashioning my steps (Proverbs 16:9).

More specifically, I found it difficult to understand why He would add years to my domestic-engineering position. It seemed He was keeping me from doing what I thought He'd planted in my heart when I was seventeen: serving Him in a public way.

At the time we married, our children ranged in age from five years old to fifteen. My new husband and I agreed that I would stay home full time to focus on raising our kids, which included homeschooling all four of them and ensuring I was able to do all I could to foster our new family relationships.

> Do not despise these small beginnings, for the LORD rejoices to see the work begin.
>
> —ZECHARIAH 4:10 (NLT)

I wish I could say it was a cakewalk. It definitely was not.

Disagreements were a daily minefield. Our children had next to nothing in common. One of our sons loved sports; the other, video games. One of our daughters was thinking about boys; the other was just learning how to color. And their personalities were just as diverse.

Most days, I felt like a referee, air traffic controller, and therapist combined.

All the while, under the surface, my heart longed to be working in church ministry. I often would pray, "When, Lord? Will I ever get to work outside the home? Will I ever be in full-time ministry?"

During those years of raising my children, I was also actively volunteering at the church we attended as a family. My husband and I both felt it was important that our kids not only saw us model a life of service , but also that they found a place where they felt comfortable serving too.

For 13 years, this was our family rhythm.

When our youngest child graduated from high school, a part-time administrative job opened up at our church. (Only God could orchestrate this perfect timing, right?) My husband knew how eager I had been to leave my life of domestic engineering behind, so when I mentioned my desire to apply for this position, I was thrilled to know I had his full support.

> **And my God will meet all your needs according to the riches of his glory in Christ Jesus.**
>
> —PHILIPPIANS 4:19 (NIV)

I got the administrative role and was giddy with excitement! I loved it and relished the opportunity to be working in ministry. Within a year and a half, another position opened up—the director of human resources. I was asked to apply. I felt completely unqualified. I prayed, sought wise counsel from trusted family and friends, and decided to go ahead and throw my hat in the ring. To my amazement, I got the job!

To be honest, even as I settled into the role, I still felt completely unqualified. I didn't have a college degree in this field or decades' worth of experience.

Or did I?

The countless hours of sibling negotiations between my children proved invaluable as I began navigating emotional personnel issues with church staff. The flurry of in-the-moment, real-time decisions came naturally to me. The many days of helping to apply Bible passages and stories to things my kids were going through translated easily to staff members who stopped by my office for leadership coaching or guidance.

I was amazed to realize that God had been actively working for years to answer my "vocational ministry" prayer! He had used my four incredible children to thoroughly prepare me for a career in human resources. And while I had been questioning my credibility and feeling like something of an imposter, God had equipped me with years of firsthand experience in the field.

It's true, I didn't have a degree, but then, I reminded myself, neither did Peter and John: "When [the rulers, elders, and scribes] observed the boldness of Peter and John and realized they were uneducated and untrained men, they were amazed and recognized that they had been with Jesus" (Acts 4:13, CSB).

> **Therefore, my beloved brothers, be steadfast, immovable, always abounding in the work of the Lord, knowing that in the Lord your labor is not in vain.**
>
> —1 CORINTHIANS 15:58 (ESV)

That verse comforted my soul. Peter and John gained life experience with Jesus, and it perfectly positioned them for the public ministry roles that God called them to. God used years of quiet, behind-the-scenes, day-to-day experiences to prepare them to use their lives in ways that would have an eternally meaningful impact on those around them.

GOD'S GIFT OF TASTE
— Buck Storm —

THE BITTER SALTINESS of tears.

A taste we all know. It starts early. A skinned knee. Maybe a broken arm. We get older. The loss of a pet. The loss of a grandparent. A parent. A spouse.

Jesus wept as well. Our tears are not futile. God keeps them in His bottle, a remembrance of this earthly pains and the promise of glory to come, when tears will end.

Jesus wept because He loves.

I imagine I will taste the salt of suffering again. But earthly seasons pass, and I'm so glad there is an eternity of joy just over the horizon.

That was what God had been beautifully doing in my life as well, all those seemingly unimportant years. I often questioned whether God really meant for me to be a mother at all. I didn't really feel very good at it. Mostly because deep down inside of me was the constant pull of desperately wanting to do something "bigger" and be involved in something that would positively change the lives of hundreds of people (not just four). I just couldn't see how He was preparing me.

Life didn't get in the way of my longing to serve Him—it paved the way for it. And I cannot think of a better way that God could have prepared me for the life of service and sacrifice He's given me.

Blessings from the Storm

Linda Marie Cumbie

The view from my apartment window looked like the opening scene from *The Wizard of Oz*. Everything in the parking lot was in motion. Sheet after sheet of rain poured and rushed over curbs, flooding streets and rocking parked cars.

It was September 2020. Hurricane Sally had arrived in Northwest Florida.

Across the sidewalk, the wind uprooted a massive oak. It lay on its side, its leaves and broken limbs blowing in the air like confetti. The storm pummeled and pushed the tree across the parking lot until it was only a few feet from my window.

The electricity went out. Darkness enveloped the parking lot, and the only light in my apartment came from the flashlight in my hand. Afraid that the tree would eventually hit the window, afraid that the rain would never stop, I prayed continuously.

I must have fallen asleep because next thing I saw was the morning sun lighting up the sky—the storm was over. I thanked God for protecting me from harm. The tree had not hit the building. It was still in the middle of the parking lot. The rugs inside my apartment were soaking wet, but I didn't think that was too bad. I ventured outside.

The building I lived in was large and designed like a hotel with over eighty apartments and four floors. Even in broad daylight, the halls were dark without electricity. The building had no generator, nor emergency lighting in the hallways. I thanked God that I had a flashlight. Once I got outside the building, the fresh air and the sight of other people were a relief.

One of the few things many say is good about a hurricane is that people see their neighbors and have time to talk and get to know each other. That morning, people sat on benches in front of the building, some scattered on the grass, and others sat on the curb of the front parking lot. In small groups, we shared our stories and talked about how thankful we were to be alive, but our gratitude was soon replaced with worry about the condition of the apartment building.

We checked our cell phones for news, listening to reports. It would be at least a week before electricity was restored, and water from the faucets had to be boiled before use. We were shocked by how bad the hurricane was in the Florida Panhandle. We had thought the area would be spared the worst of it. As each new report brought word of more destruction, we began to have a real sense of the extent of this storm. The bridges to the beach were damaged, and repairs were expected to take nearly a year.

At several grocery stores, the national guard was distributing truckloads of ice and water for those in need. Since my phone had to be charged in my car, I decided to try to drive to the store. When I went back to my apartment to get my purse, I discovered that the flooding from the top three floors had run down the walls and into my living room and bedrooms. Worse, the people above me must have had pets that had accidents.

With the exception of one small window, the windows in my apartment were not the kind that could be opened for air.

With no electricity or ventilation, the smell was so strong that my eyes began to sting and breathing was difficult.

On my way to the store, I saw people already up on ladders putting blue tarps over their roofs that would need to be replaced. I could hear the sounds of chain saws whirring. Restoration was beginning, but most of the traffic lights were out. Driving was a cautious affair.

My family lived in another state, and I had talked to them earlier. They were praying for me. I called again and told my brother about my apartment.

He said, "You can't stay there. I'll get on the computer and find an Airbnb for you." As we talked on the phone, I waited in line at the grocery store for the ice and water, and he searched the internet. Place after place was without power or, if they had power, had no vacancies.

> I waited patiently for the LORD; he turned to me and heard my cry. He lifted me out of the slimy pit, out of the mud and mire; he set my feet on a rock and gave me a firm place to stand.
>
> —PSALM 40:1–2 (NIV)

Eventually, he did find a suitable Airbnb, a garage apartment situated next to a large house that the owners also rented. This was a miracle.

I bought water and ice for my neighbors and then went back to the apartment, where I packed a small suitcase and grabbed my renter's insurance policy. The Airbnb was only available for 3 days, and my brother had paid the fee. The owners gave him the combination for the lockbox on the door.

When I reached the apartment and went inside, I was so grateful. It was a lovely space, with a small kitchen area, a queen-size bed, a large television, and—best of all—electricity, clean water, and air conditioning!

When I looked at my renter's policy, I could not believe my good fortune. The policy covered alternate housing in the case of a disaster. The next morning, I called my insurance company and was assigned an adjuster. They said she would contact me soon.

I returned to my old apartment building. After seeing how quickly people were rallying to repair damage to their homes, I thought surely my apartment complex would work quickly to correct the damage to our units.

The apartment manager said she had a restoration service coming in, and they would vacuum out the water from my carpets. I told her the carpet needed to be replaced. She went into my apartment and sprayed some kind of cherry deodorizer that she said smelled great, but when I went in, the smell was putrid. It now smelled like cherry-scented animal waste.

I told the apartment manager that my renter's insurance would cover alternate housing for me while they did the repairs. I could not believe it when she said the apartment was livable. Thus began a 60-day battle to have my apartment repaired and restored. But it was also 60 days of seeing God's blessings and provisions for me.

I went back to the Airbnb. I called my insurance company again but still did not talk to my assigned adjuster. I met the owners of the Airbnb, Carol and Kent, when they stopped by to see if I needed anything. Kent only stayed for a few minutes, but when Carol and I started to talk, we found we had a lot in common. She also loved to write and had been a professional journalist for many years.

When it was time for me to check out, Carol came by and said that she and Kent had talked and prayed. They had a room in their house that I could rent until my apartment repairs were complete. She said they knew it could take time for the insurance to pay. When I got my insurance money, I could give them the back rent.

It was a great blessing to me, and also a great leap of faith on all of our parts. We really didn't know each other, and yet it seemed as if we had been friends for years. In the evenings we watched TV and the three of us had wonderful conversations. Kent liked to bake and would always make some kind of chocolate cookies or cake. They said it was like having a sibling in the house, which made me realize how much I'd been missing the sense of family. We became lifelong friends.

On one hand, I could see how God was blessing me; on the other hand, I was anxious. I had

> **The angel of the LORD encamps around those who fear him, and he delivers them.**
>
> **—PSALM 34:7 (NIV)**

gone back to work, and living out of a suitcase was difficult. I called and called my adjuster and still could not reach her. I worried that my renter's policy would not pay. Each day I went to my apartment and took pictures to document the damage. The restoration company had come in to set up huge fans to dry the carpet, but it still smelled terrible. The drywall had been cut in several areas, revealing mold inside the walls. This process continued for weeks. I had to pay October's rent for an apartment I still couldn't live in, and there seemed to be no end in sight.

Had I not met Carol and Kent, I would not have known about getting a public adjuster, an insurance professional who works for the policyholder, advocating on his or her behalf to help settle claims; on their advice, I enlisted one. At first it seemed that even he was not making any headway. Three weeks into November things had still not been resolved, and my rent would be due for December. I felt I was running out of time. I continued to pray, discouraged that God had not intervened.

And then, in the final week of November, astonishing things began to happen.

For the grace of God has appeared that offers salvation to all people.

—TITUS 2:11 (NIV)

The insurance company sent several checks for my living expenses and losses. When I went to my apartment for my daily inspection, I saw that the kitchen was flooded and the sink was filled with rancid food. Someone upstairs had poured grease in their sink, which had somehow flooded my kitchen. I went to the apartment manager's office. This time, even she had to admit the apartment was unlivable, and she released me from my lease.

As I left, one of my neighbors told me about a new building just a few streets away that I should look at. It was beautiful, with an Olympic-size pool and exercise room. That manager told me I needed to apply immediately because there were only three units left, so I filled out the paperwork on the spot and was approved. Then he said that he and a friend were helping people move their belongings. They had only one morning open that they could move me, Wednesday, November 25.

A day later, I stood in the middle of my living room, breathing in the clean smell of a new apartment and admiring all its special amenities. It was so much nicer than my old apartment. Even through the storm, God had blessed me in ways I could not imagine, and I was filled with awe and gratitude. His timing was perfect—it was Thanksgiving Day!

Something Old, Loved, and Tattered

Lynne Hartke

"How tall are the mountains we're hiking today?" I asked my husband, Kevin, as we enjoyed a traditional Irish breakfast—porridge, sausages, black pudding, eggs, and grilled tomatoes. We were visiting Ireland as a partnership program between Tullamore, Ireland, and our city of Chandler, Arizona, where my husband worked in local government. Knowing our love of nature, the trip organizers had arranged a morning hike for us with an area guide and storyteller.

Kevin slathered rich Irish butter on a slice of soda bread. "It's 1,729 feet."

I choked on my morning tea. "Seventeen hundred feet! Sounds more like a hill than a mountain."

"Careful now," Kevin cautioned, casting a worried look at the locals dining around us.

I had no desire to be insensitive but struggled to swallow my disappointment. Didn't the organizers know we had the towering 14,000-foot peaks of the Rocky Mountains in the States? And didn't they realize we had hiked a 19,000-foot volcano in Peru the summer before? A climb of 1,729 feet didn't seem like much of a challenge.

I had arrived in Ireland with high expectations of memory-making adventures, majestic castles, ocean-sprayed beaches, and eclectic souvenir shops. After spending over three decades in the same house, in the same Arizona city, my humdrum life needed a jump-start.

But instead—on our first break from official meetings—we were going on a stroll through some tired-out, grandparent-appropriate mountains. And with a guide, nonetheless, so we couldn't hurry through the morning and get onto more exciting activities.

I attempted to tuck my grumbling attitude in my back pocket when we met our guide, John, at the trailhead. Dressed in khaki shorts, a loose T-shirt, and hiking boots, he looked prepared for the day, his cropped white hair the only hint of his 70 years. John grabbed his walking stick, a staff he had chosen from a hazel tree with a crook at the top. The stick looked as worn as the mountains behind him.

> **This is what the LORD says: "Stand by the ways and see and ask for the ancient paths, where the good way is, and walk in it; then you will find a resting place for your souls."**
>
> **—JEREMIAH 6:16 (NASB)**

"We'll have a bit of adventure today," he promised.

"We'll see," I muttered as I grabbed my water bottle.

With a slight warning glance, Kevin slung a day pack over his shoulder as we set off on a wide path, packed down from years of footsteps.

Within minutes we walked under canopied trees that could have been a rehearsed advertisement for all the greens of Ireland, giving validation to its nickname, the Emerald Isle.

Ferns. Leaves. Moss. Ivy. Holly.

Green above us. Green below us. Green around us. If color had a noise, we had stepped into surround-sound green. Under the shade of an ancient oak tree, I noticed shamrocks, the first I had seen outside a nature book. Irish shamrocks!

"Don't wait for me. I'll catch up," I said, pulling my camera from my pocket. Kevin was used to my tendency to stop and take photos and then jog up to join him, but John was not. He stopped. Waited. And told a story.

"Ah, yes, 'tis the shamrock," he began in his Irish brogue. "The real shamrock and not the clover that some people say St. Patrick used to talk about the Trinity, the three leaves of Father, Son, and Holy Spirit."

John leaned on his walking staff, settling into his role as a trained storyteller. "Let me tell you why. This is the wood sorrel, which grows all over the woods of Ireland. This is the true shamrock that St. Patrick most likely used in his story."

My interest was piqued. Maybe the morning wouldn't be so boring after all. I opened a notebook and began taking detailed notes when we stopped at different points along the way. At each stop, John told us stories about the plants we encountered as we walked through the woodland to a waterfall and then through a flower-covered meadow to a blanket bog.

John began each story with the phrase, "I will tell you why." He went on to describe the ancient medicinal uses of many plants, declaring, "God has given them for our benefit."

He introduced us to a purple flower, similar in appearance to a small thistle. Known as devil's bit scabies, the plant held so many healing properties, according to John, that the devil came down and bit it off close to the ground, giving it a shallow root system. Yellow pimpernel, a five-petaled flower, whose Irish name means laughter, was center stage as a remedy for depression.

We learned another sweet-scented yellow flower—bedstraw—was once used to stuff mattresses. John had remedies for aches and pains, for sickness, and even bad breath. Every plant had a story, some tales dating back to the fourth century AD.

The hours of the morning disappeared, but we didn't notice as butterflies fluttered around us—a meadow brown, a cabbage white, and an orange-and-brown peacock butterfly, with spectacular blue eyes on the hind wings. At the summit—all 1,729 feet—we sat down for a simple lunch, surrounded by heather and a yellow plant I had seen growing along the roadways.

"Ragwort," John said, fingering the fragile petals. "People say that fairies ride it through the forests."

I wasn't so sure about the fairies, but I knew one thing. I had arrived in Ireland thinking my life was tedious after living in the same house, in the same city, for more than 30 years, but listening to John, I discovered a sense of place, centuries deep, that I could not fathom. John wore it all as comfortably as his worn-in boots, as he shared ancient stories of legend and mystery, where even the flowers had a part to play in the tales.

> **Join together in following my example, brothers and sisters, and just as you have us as a model, keep your eyes on those who live as we do.**
>
> **—PHILIPPIANS 3:17 (NIV)**

"Do you have a book you would recommend that contains stories of the plants and flowers of Ireland?" I asked John on our way back.

"I have one at my house," he said. "Do you have time to stop?"

"Sure," we exclaimed, no longer concerned about time.

While John showed us his garden and talked of his plans since retiring, I was thankful the day had turned out to be more than I could have imagined. Through an Irish storyteller, God had shown me kindness despite my stinking attitude.

And the kindnesses that day were not over.

As promised, John handed me a book of herbs and healing plants of Ireland.

I turned over the tattered volume in my hands. The pages were water-stained and dog-eared, with random corners turned down. As a lover of books who reluctantly lends her favorites for fear they won't be returned, I understood the value of the gift I had been given.

> See how the flowers of the field grow. They do not labor or spin. Yet I tell you that not even Solomon in all his splendor was dressed like one of these. If that is how God clothes the grass of the field . . . will he not much more clothe you—you of little faith?
>
> —MATTHEW 6:28–30 (NIV)

"This is a much-loved copy," I said, quietly, smoothing the blue cover.

"I have gotten everything I am needing out of it," John said. He smiled. "And I can buy another."

GOD'S GIFT OF SMELL
— Heidi Gaul —

AROMATHERAPY IS ACCEPTED as a safe, natural treatment for an assortment of conditions. Scientists at the Stevens Institute of Technology have found a connection between the scent of coffee and the ability to focus, while research at Ohio State University has linked the essence of lemon with the ability to make decisions more easily. Lavender, mint, and clary sage, among others, have all earned a place in the essential oil cabinet. We can thank Jesus, our Great Physician, for blessing us with these beneficial scented oils and put them to good use.

I felt like he just handed me 20 years of his life. His passion. His love. His stories.

"Many of my stories are from this book," he continued. "If I had known you would be wanting it, I would have gotten you a new copy."

I laughed at his turn of the phrase, shook my head, and thanked him one more time. "I didn't know I would be wanting it until I met you."

John's phrase lingered as we said goodbye and drove back to the hotel. What would people be wanting after spending a day with me? What would they carry away in their hands?

Turning the faded pages of John's gift, I determined to not always search for new heights of excitement but to find treasure on familiar paths. Sometimes something old, loved, and tattered is the most valuable gift of all.

The Divine Appointment

Andrea Herzer

The smell of rubbing alcohol filled the surgical center as I awaited my procedure. Other patients furtively glanced at me as they carefully avoided my walker in the small waiting room. To their credit, it was difficult not to stare at the large black coccyx cushion that filled the seat beneath me. With a veneer of politeness, they pretended not to notice my feet, purple and swollen, propped up on the walker. I wanted to go home—away from questioning glances—and return to the comfort of my bed. Embarrassed, I shifted in my seat and looked determinedly at my lap.

I was 39 years old and a married stay-at-home mother of three children when I developed the neuroimmune disease that changed all of our lives. Complex regional pain syndrome (CRPS) is agonizingly painful and typically begins after surgery or trauma to a limb. In my case, a golf-cart accident and subsequent surgery triggered this disabling disease in my (dominant) left hand. Then, as it often does, CRPS spread to my other limbs. Within a year, even after countless nerve blocks and epidurals, I could not walk without a walker.

My active family and church life ended when I became bedridden. Excruciating pain kept me from sleeping; the disease ignited a burning fire throughout my body. I did not understand why God allowed me to suffer this way. Through faith, I embraced the Bible's promise that "in all things God works for the good of those who love him, who have been called according to his purpose" (Romans 8:28, NIV).

Every seat in the waiting room was taken, but it was eerily silent—except for the tall woman in the wheelchair. She sat in the center of the room, loudly talking to herself, humming, and trying to make eye contact with others. Her halo of orange hair contrasted with her purple lipstick. Thick glasses magnified her blue eyes as she looked pleadingly around the room and sucked on a lollipop that likely contained pain medication.

> **Be devoted to one another in love. Honor one another above yourselves.**
>
> —ROMANS 12:10 (NIV)

Everyone in that small waiting area was careful to look away, including me. After all, I was in tremendous pain, anxious about my upcoming IV and procedure, and simply wanted to sit in silence. I even said a quick prayer, "Lord, please help her to stop talking so loudly."

But the Lord firmly spoke to my spirit. *Andrea, why aren't you showing My love to My child?*

Immediately, I felt God's great tenderness and compassion toward this woman. I asked the Lord's forgiveness and then asked Him to help me reach out to her in love.

The next time she shouted a question and looked around for attention, I met her eyes, answered her, and smiled. She beamed right back at me. The tension in the room dissolved as we began to talk to each other. Other people in the waiting room visibly relaxed. They met my eyes with slight smiles and seemed grateful that the woman's attention was directed toward me instead of them.

God's loving presence, guidance, and conviction in that surgery center ultimately changed my life. I learned that the woman in the wheelchair was named Kathy, and she was afflicted with a disease that had necessitated the amputation of her lower legs and her fingers. Her husband had divorced her after the first amputation, so she lived alone and had little support.

As we continued to speak, Kathy dug through her small purse, but the objects within kept falling out. She was distressed because she could not lean over to pick them up.

> **Follow God's example, therefore, as dearly loved children and walk in the way of love, just as Christ loved us and gave himself up for us as a fragrant offering and sacrifice to God.**
>
> **—EPHESIANS 5:1–2 (NIV)**

I wanted to help her solve this problem, and immediately thought of a sizeable orange handbag that I'd recently purchased but never used. Since one of the nurses, delighted to witness our conversation, had shared that we had the same appointment schedule, I brought the purse to my next appointment. Kathy was already there when I checked in, and she began to cry when I handed it to her. She showed it off to all the medical staff. Her love and gratitude humbled me.

On our next medical visit, Kathy brought me a gift bag with a card. Inside the small bag, surrounded by crumpled tissue paper, was a small dust-covered angel figurine. Kathy told me that she had given me one of her treasures to show how much she treasured me. A gesture of kindness that cost me so little meant everything to her. She generously sacrificed one of her few possessions to express her gratitude.

Kathy is gone now, but my few encounters with her were life-changing. She was a strong and loving woman who suffered greatly, and meeting her changed my perspective on my own health issues. I began to recognize and give thanks for my many blessings. My eyes were opened to how God's goodness was still evident in my life.

> **Be completely humble and gentle; be patient, bearing with one another in love.**
>
> —EPHESIANS 4:2 (NIV)

I now try to notice when someone else seems lonely or fearful during a medical appointment. Health issues are isolating, so I make eye contact and smile at patients who are sitting alone. Like Kathy, they deserve to know that someone sees them and values them. Sometimes a person may just need a kind or encouraging word. Other times, after a conversation, I offer to pray with them. It never hurts to ask, and no one has ever declined a prayer.

Kathy was an unexpected but life-changing blessing. My encounters with her restored my perspective, reignited my joy, and began to reveal my calling. After decades of suffering from ongoing debilitating health issues, including cancer, my ministry to others with health issues is one of the greatest joys of my life. But my calling did not begin with my first diagnosis or even my second or third diagnosis. It started with the Great Physician's prescription to show His love to someone who suffered.

The Wonder of Mayflies

Jennie Ivey

I couldn't remember when I'd ever been so tired. Worn out from work, worry, and too many family and community obligations, I looked forward to spending a few late-summer days swimming, canoeing, and just plain relaxing at my friend Connie's lake cabin. I arrived after dark the first evening and enjoyed a wonderful supper with the handful of friends gathered there. Then I collapsed into bed for the best night's sleep I'd experienced in a long time.

The next morning, with a steaming mug of coffee in hand, I headed down the gently sloping backyard to the boat dock to watch the sun come up. To my chagrin, swarms of insects so thick that I could barely see the lake engulfed me as I neared the dock. There appeared to be thousands of them. Perhaps millions. These hideous-looking bugs were on the grass and in the trees. They landed on my clothes and in my hair. Worst of all, one of them plopped into my coffee.

Trying not to scream or gag, I whirled around and scurried back to the safety of the cabin.

Connie was grinning as I entered the screened porch, showing her the insect in my coffee cup. "I forgot to tell you last night that you'd arrived just in time for the mayfly hatch," she said.

"Is that what these awful creatures are?" I asked.

"Come on in and let's get you some new coffee," she said. "Then we'll talk."

I knew I should be a good sport and act as if this was no big deal. But how? I was only going to be there for a few days and, from the looks of things, I wouldn't be able to enjoy the lake at all. Mayflies had stolen my vacation from me.

I wanted to shake my fists at the sky. But maybe, I told myself, it would be better to say a quick prayer, though I wasn't sure God wanted to hear me rant and rave about bugs. But I've always trusted that He's okay when we share our frustrations and even our anger with Him. So before I headed to the kitchen to get a clean mug and some mayfly-free coffee, I closed my eyes and whispered these words: "What's up with this pestilence of insects, Lord? They're going to ruin my vacation for sure. Please, please, *please* make them go away."

> **The heavens declare the glory of God; the skies proclaim the work of his hands.**
>
> —PSALM 19:1 (NIV)

Connie was pulling a pan of chocolate-chip muffins from the oven when I walked into the kitchen. She placed a couple of them on a plate and handed it to me. "Let's go out to the porch and I'll tell you what I know about mayflies," she said.

First off, she assured me that mayflies are nothing like locusts. "They don't destroy crops or landscaping," she said. "In fact, by the time they hatch, they've already eaten their last meal."

Hmm, I thought. *I wonder how that works.*

Connie also told me that mayflies don't bite or sting and that their presence near bodies of water is a sign that the ecosystem is healthy. "When we finish breakfast, we'll take my binoculars out to the yard and you can see the mayflies up close," she said. A few minutes later, we dragged folding lawn chairs about halfway down to the dock and set them up just above where the swarm started.

"Take a look," Connie said, handing me the binoculars.

The posts that supported the dock's roof were covered in spiderwebs. The rafters were covered in spiderwebs. The wooden Adirondack chairs that faced out into open water were covered with spiderwebs. The dock was positively furry with spiderwebs! And caught in those webs were mayflies too numerous to count. I zoomed in and focused the binoculars so that I could study the insects. Mayflies are about an inch long and have thin, grayish-brown bodies and delicate gossamer wings. It made me feel kind of sad to see them trapped, though I know that spiders—like all God's creatures—must eat to survive.

But equally as amazing as the spiderwebs were the dozens of birds perched on the long electric line running from the house to the dock. They were all facing the water.

"What kind of birds are those?" I asked.

"Tree swallows," Connie told me as I trained the binoculars on them. They're beautiful birds, with iridescent blue-green backs and white fronts that make them look as though they're wearing a tuxedo. Like other types of swallows, tree swallows have forked tails.

"No surprise that they feed on insects, right?" Connie said. "I've heard that each bird eats about two thousand bugs in one day."

"Then why are they sitting on that wire instead of hunting?" I asked.

"Every living thing has to rest," she said with a laugh, and with that, we each adjusted our chairs to the reclining position and closed our eyes. It was glorious. We made good use of the screened porch that afternoon, sipping iced tea and playing cards, and working on a jigsaw puzzle, talking and laughing all the while. As the sun moved lower in the sky, Connie suggested we take the canoe out to explore the lake.

"We'll have to walk through the mayflies to get there, right?" I said, clearly not relishing the thought.

"Yep," she said with a smile. "But remember—they don't bite or sting. You'll be okay." Dressed in swimsuits and flip-flops, we headed out the door and down the lawn. The mayflies seemed to be swarming even more densely than they had that morning. They hovered near my face and lit on my nose and ears. I clamped my mouth shut, shuddering at the thought of swallowing a mayfly. I cheered when I smacked two with one blow after they landed on the back of my neck.

> **Worship the LORD in the splendor of his holiness; tremble before him, all the earth.**
>
> **—PSALM 96:9 (NIV)**

That's when I noticed that Connie wasn't smiling. "I know they're irritating," she said, "but I can't bear to kill one."

"How come?" I asked. "They don't exactly seem like an endangered species."

She shook her head. "No, they're not. But they only get the chance to live 24 hours in this beautiful world. I hate to take any of those hours away from them if I can help it." We untied the canoe from the tree trunk where it was secured, flipped it over, and scrambled aboard as it slipped into the water. We didn't have to paddle very far from shore before we'd left the mayflies behind.

Connie continued her lesson. "Mayfly nymphs spend most of their lives, sometimes as long as 2 years, on the bottom of lakes and rivers," she told me. "When they finally get their wings, they fly out of the water in a colossal cloud and molt one more time. It's called the hatch and it's what we're seeing now." She went on to explain that mayfly mating happens right above shallow water. Males swarm over the lake and females fly into the swarm to be fertilized. They lay eggs while hovering over the water, and those eggs sink to the bottom. Then the cycle begins again.

But ask the animals, and they will teach you, or the birds in the sky, and they will tell you. In his hand is the life of every creature and the breath of all mankind.

—JOB 12:7, 10 (NIV)

"So these mayflies we're seeing are knocking on heaven's door right now," I said, suddenly understanding. Wow. No wonder Connie didn't want to kill them.

"Right," she said. "Those that don't die of old age become food for spiders and fish and other predators." She pointed to the sky over the boat dock. "Take a look."

I didn't need binoculars to see that hundreds of tree swallows, perhaps some of the same ones that had been perched on the electric line that morning, were swooping through the swarm of mayflies, eating their fill. It was one of the most beautiful and acrobatic nature dances I'd ever witnessed.

Connie and I sat there in that gently rocking canoe, paddles resting across our laps, and watched for a long, long time.

GOD'S GIFT OF SIGHT

— Lynne Hartke —

FRANCIS CHICKERING KNEW the power of detailed observation. A minister's wife in Maine in the 1860s, Francis became fascinated with the snowflakes on her windowsill. After collecting the flakes on dark material, she memorized their structure under a magnifying glass, and then cut out their shapes from paper. She later published one of the first books on snowflakes: *Cloud Crystals, A Snowflake Album*. Her collection revealed what the naked eye could not see—the unique, detailed beauty of this part of God's creation. Nothing is too small for His perfect design. Even a tiny snowflake.

We talked about the food chain. We talked about the seasons of the year and about life cycles. We talked about how grateful we were to witness and be part of God's perfect design for this world. And as we talked, I came to understand that being at Connie's lake cabin during the mayfly hatch wasn't a bother or an inconvenience. It wasn't bad timing and it hadn't ruined my vacation. In fact, it was a gift.

A gift I'll cherish for as long as I live.

Contributors

A Note from the Editors

We hope you enjoyed *Blessed by His Love,* published by Guideposts. For over 75 years, Guideposts, a nonprofit organization, has been driven by a vision of a world filled with hope. We aspire to be the voice of a trusted friend, a friend who makes you feel more hopeful and connected.

By making a purchase from Guideposts, you join our community in touching millions of lives, inspiring them to believe that all things are possible through faith, hope, and prayer. Your continued support allows us to provide uplifting resources to those in need. Whether through our communities, websites, apps, or publications, we inspire our audiences, bring them together, and comfort, uplift, entertain, and guide them. Visit us at guideposts.org to learn more.

We would love to hear from you. Write us at Guideposts, P.O. Box 5815, Harlan, Iowa 51593 or call us at (800) 932-2145. Did you love *Blessed by His Love*? Leave a review for this product on guideposts.org/shop. Your feedback helps others in our community find relevant products.

Find inspiration, find faith, find Guideposts.

Shop our best sellers and favorites at
guideposts.org/shop

Or scan the QR code to go directly to our Shop